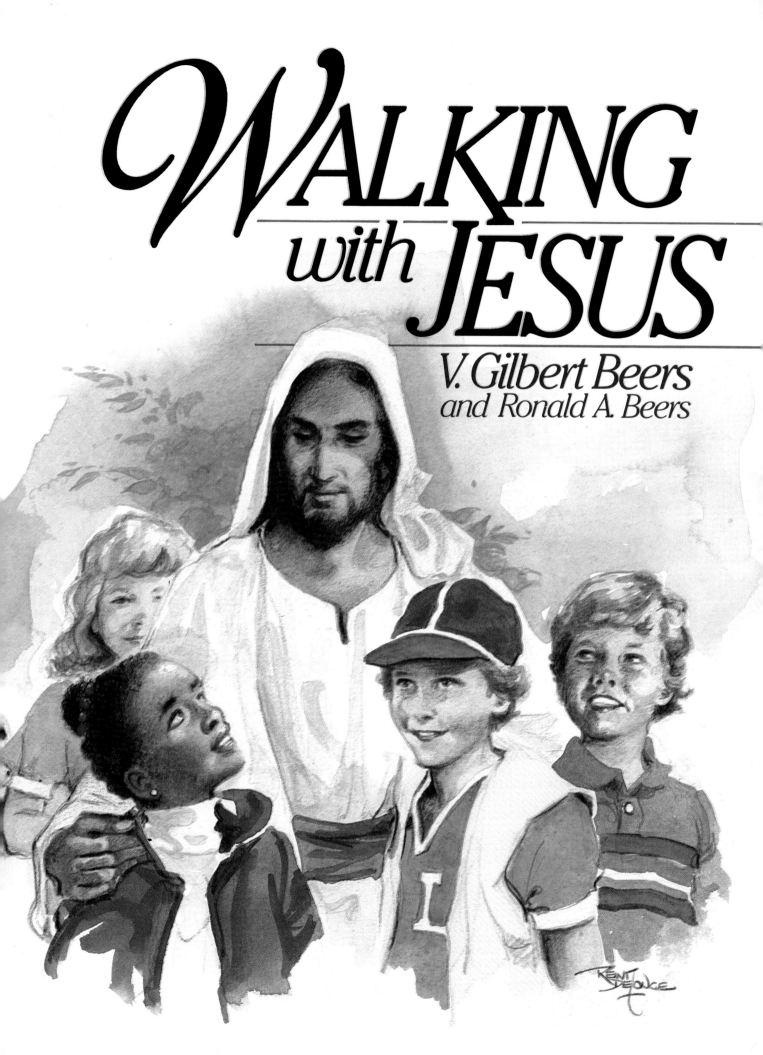

Walking with Jesus

V. Gilbert Beers
and Ronald A. Beers

TO PARENTS AND TEACHERS

One of the highest goals we as parents and teachers can set for our children is to be more like Jesus. This book is designed to help you guide your child toward becoming more Christlike. It is the life of Jesus, presented through a retelling of the most significant stories about Him. Each story focuses on one quality seen in the Lord Jesus, a quality which we as parents or teachers desire for our children.

A Think, Learn, and Do section helps the child see that Christlike quality in Jesus, and see it as a goal for his or her own life. It also offers a practical way to put that quality to work in daily living.

In the back you will find a guide to the Christlike qualities taught in this book.

WALKING WITH JESUS
by V. Gilbert Beers and Ronald A. Beers

Illustrations by Reint De Jonge

Published by
HERE'S LIFE PUBLISHERS, INC.
P.O. Box 1576
San Bernardino, CA 92402   U.S.A.

Library of Congress Catalogue Card 84-047804
ISBN 0-89840-069-4
HLP Product No. 950873
Copyright 1984 V. Gilbert Beers and Ronald A. Beers

Illustrations selected from:
    Het Evangelie Naar Johannes,
      published by Stichting De Evangelische Omroep, The Netherlands
    Kinderbijbel Het Nieuwe Testament,
      published by Boekencentrum b.v., The Netherlands
    Kinderbijbel
      published by Boekencentrum b.v., The Netherlands

Printed in the United States of America.

CONTENTS

JESUS LIVED BEFORE
Like Jesus: TO LIVE IN HEAVEN

The stories in this book are about Jesus and the many things that He did while He was here on earth. Some stories tell how He raised people from the dead, or helped blind people see again, or told people about heaven.

Before anything else existed, there was Christ, with God. He has always been alive and is Himself God. He created everything there is — nothing exists that He didn't make. John 1:1-3

If you think Jesus is just an ordinary man, you will wonder how these stories could have happened. Ordinary people like you and your friends do not do these things.

But Jesus could. That's because He is God's Son. Jesus knows about heaven because He lived there for thousands of years before He came to earth one night in Bethlehem. Jesus was there with God when the world was made. He was there with God when people were made. God and Jesus were the same.

The Bible says nothing was made without Jesus' help. Jesus helped give life to anything that is alive.

Since Jesus made life, that's why He could heal sick people, or help blind people see, or crippled people walk.

Jesus can even help people come back to life. Jesus is also able to take us into His home in heaven when we die. There we will live with Him forever.

Of course, some of these things are hard to understand. But as you read the stories in this book, remember that Jesus is God who came to earth into a human body. He is called God's Son because He was God on earth, God living among people, showing us what God is like.

So if you and I are puzzled about some of the stories to come, remember who Jesus is. And remember where He lived through all those years.

Think

1. Who is Jesus? 2. Where did Jesus live before He came to earth?
3. Why is Jesus called God's Son? 4. Why can Jesus tell you about heaven and about God?

John 1:1-5

Learn

From this story we learn that Jesus lived in heaven before He came to earth and that He is God.

Do

From one of your Sunday school papers, cut out a picture of Jesus. Paste it on a larger yellow paper circle. When you look at the picture, remember that Jesus lived in heaven, and lives there today.

JESUS, GOD'S SPECIAL GIFT

Like Jesus: A GIFT THAT WILL BE GIVEN

One day the Angel Gabriel made a special visit to a little town called Nazareth. He appeared suddenly in Mary's house, shining so bright it was hard to look at him.

"You are a special person," the angel told Mary. "God is pleased with you!"

Of course Mary was afraid, as you would be. Why would an angel come to see her?

"Don't be afraid," the angel said. "God is going to give you a special gift. Soon you will have a baby boy, and will call Him Jesus. He will be God's own Son, a great King who will live forever."

"But how can this be?" Mary asked the angel. Mary did not even have a husband, so how could she have a baby?

"God will be the father of this baby" the angel told Mary. "God will do this because He has promised that He would."

Now, Mary was sure that God really would give her this special baby. Some gifts are like that. You KNOW you will get them because someone you trust has said that you will.

Suddenly the angel was gone. Mary bowed her head and thanked God for this wonderful promise. She knew God would give this special son just as the angel said.

Mary was so happy that she went to tell the good news to her cousin, Elizabeth, who was also going to have a baby. Together they spent many days, talking about the special children God was giving to them.

Gabriel appeared to her and said, "Congratulations, favored lady! The Lord is with You!"...Mary said, "I am the Lord's servant, and I am willing to do whatever He wants." Luke 1:28,38

Think

1. What special gift did the angel say Mary would receive? 2. Why did Mary know she would receive this gift? 3. When someone you trust says you will get a gift, why do you know you will get it?

Learn

From this story we learn that God gives each special gift He promises.

Do

Make a list of five gifts God will give you tomorrow, such as food, water, or your home. How do you know you will receive them? Thank God for these gifts.

JESUS IS BORN

Like Jesus: A PROMISE KEPT

J oseph loved Mary and wanted her to be his wife. But one day he learned that she was going to have a baby. And how could Joseph marry her now. Who was the father of Mary's baby?

That night Joseph lay in bed, wondering what to do. Suddenly an angel appeared in his room. "Ask Mary to be your wife," the angel said. "Her baby is God's Son. You will call Him Jesus, for God promised long ago to send Him to save people from their sins. Then they may live in heaven with Him."

The angel went away as quickly as he had come. Joseph sat up in bed, thinking about the things he had seen and heard. He was happy now, for he could ask Mary to be his wife. He knew now that her baby was God's special promise.

After they were married, Joseph and Mary lived in Nazareth, where Joseph had grown up as a boy. He was a carpenter, so he kept busy making carts, wooden spoons, and many other things from wood. He did this for all the neighbors around him.

One day Joseph was busily working when he heard some bad news. The Roman emperor wanted to make a list of all the people in the land. The emperor said that everyone had to return to the place where their grandfathers or great-grandfathers had lived. There they would put their names on the emperor's list.

Joseph would have to go to Bethlehem, where one of his great-great-great-great-grandfathers, King David, had lived. Mary was about to have her baby, so it was a very bad time for her to travel. But Joseph and Mary had to do what the emperor said.

Before long, Mary and Joseph headed for Bethlehem. In those days, people traveled in groups called caravans so that thieves could not hurt them.

After many days, Joseph and Mary arrived in Bethlehem. Mary was tired and ready to rest. Joseph tried hard to find a place to stay.

But the inn in Bethlehem was full. There was no other place to stay either. There was no place except the stable behind the inn.

That night Mary's baby was born in that stable. The cows and donkeys must have watched as Mary wrapped her baby in strips of cloth and laid Him in a manger.

What a special night! Mary knew that God's promise had come true.

It was also a special night for some shepherds who sat warming themselves by a fire on a hillside outside the town. The stars

The Savior...has been born tonight in Bethlehem! How will you recognize Him? You will find a baby wrapped in a blanket, lying in a manger!" Luke 2:11,12

On the night that Jesus was born angels announced His birth to shepherds on the hillsides near Bethlehem. The Bible mentions sheep more often than any other animal. Sheep would never fight another animal, so the shepherds were always on the lookout for wild animals which might attack the sheep.

twinkled and nearby were their sleeping sheep.

Suddenly the night sky burst forth with a bright light and an angel stood nearby. Of course, the shepherds were terrified.

"Don't be afraid. I have wonderful news for you," the angel said. "Tonight, in Bethlehem, God's Son was born. He is the one who will save the world from its sins."

The shepherds listened carefully as the angel talked. "Hurry down to the village and you will find the baby in a stable, wrapped in strips of cloth," the angel said.

Suddenly the sky was filled with angels, praising God together. "Glory to God, and peace on earth for those who please Him," they said. Then the angels disappeared. Once again only the stars filled the night sky.

The shepherds were filled with wonder as they hurried down the hillsides and into the town. When they reached the stable, they found Mary, Joseph, and Baby Jesus, just as the angel had said. Then the shepherds knelt and worshiped Jesus before they left. And of course they told others about Him.

Mary thought much about God's promise to send this special son. Surely she must have thanked Him many times that night for keeping His promise!

The shepherds told everyone what had happened and what the angel had said to them about this child. All who heard the shepherds' story expressed astonishment, but Mary quietly treasured these things in her heart and often thought about them. Luke 2:17-19

Think

1. To whom had God promised to send Baby Jesus? 2. What promise did God send His angels to make to the shepherds? 3. How did God keep His promise?

Learn

From this story we learn that God kept His promise to send Jesus to earth.

Do

What do people think of those who do not keep their promises? Make a list of three promises you have made. Ask God to help you keep your promises.

SIMEON AND ANNA

Like Jesus: WORTH WAITING FOR

How long would you wait for a friend to meet you? How long would you wait for someone in your family? What about a king, or a queen? Would you wait a long time to see them?

Simeon and Anna waited for many years to see Baby Jesus. They lived in Jerusalem and heard many things about this wonderful Person who would come some day. They knew that God had promised to send His Son and He would save His people from their sins.

God had even told Simeon that he would not die until he had seen Baby Jesus. Although Simeon was an old man, he believed God and waited patiently for that wonderful day.

Then one day God told Simeon to go to God's house. "Perhaps this is the day I have waited for," Simeon thought as he hurried toward God's house.

Simeon sat on the stone steps and waited some more. Then Mary and Joseph walked into the courtyard holding a baby. They had brought Baby Jesus to be dedicated. Somehow Simeon knew that Baby Jesus was God's Son. Simeon's long wait was over!

Simeon rushed across the courtyard, took Jesus into his arms and praised God. "Now I can die in peace," he said. "Now I have seen God's Son."

About that time Anna, an old woman who lived there at God's house, ran over to Baby Jesus. She also praised God that she had seen His Son.

These two people had waited many years to see Baby Jesus. You can see why they were so happy that they had seen Him at last. After all, Jesus is Someone worth waiting for, isn't He?

Think

1. Who waited many years to see Jesus? 2. Why do you think they were so happy to see Him? 3. Are you glad to wait for someone or something worth waiting for? Why? 4. When people wait for you, do you make them feel glad they waited for you? How?

"Lord," [Simeon] said, "now I can die content! For I have seen Him as you promised me I would. I have seen the Savior You have given to the world. He is the Light that will shine upon the nations, and He will be the glory of Your people Israel!" Luke 2:29-32

Learn

From this story we learn that Simeon and Anna waited many years to see Jesus and they were glad to wait to see Him.

Do

The next time you must wait for someone you love, think of two words — Simeon and Anna.

WISE MEN VISIT JESUS

Like Jesus: DESERVING GOOD GIFTS

In a land far away, some wise men watched the night sky. They often watched the stars, for they thought the stars told them many things.

On this night these men saw something unusual. A new star was shining, bigger and more beautiful than any star they had ever seen.

"This must be a sign that a great King has been born," they said. "He is a King greater than all others."

Of course the wise men wanted to follow the star. Perhaps it would lead them to this great King.

Night after night the men traveled, following the new star. At last the wise men came to the land of Israel. They went straight to the city where King Herod lived.

"Where is this new King?" they asked. "We have seen His star and want to worship Him."

King Herod did not like to hear about a new king. He was king. If a new king was born, what would happen to him?

King Herod called his own wise men and religious leaders and asked where this King would be born.

"In Bethlehem," they answered.

"Go and find Him," Herod told the wise men. "When you do, tell me where I may find him. I want to worship Him, too." Of course he wanted to kill Jesus, not worship Him.

The wise men went to Bethlehem. When they found Jesus, they gave Him special gifts, for He was a special person.

Then God warned the wise men not to tell Herod about Jesus. So they went home another way, praising and thanking God for helping them find Jesus. They were glad they could give their special gifts to this special person. Aren't you?

They opened their presents and gave Him gold, frankinsense and myrrh. But when they returned to their own land, they didn't go through Jerusalem to report to Herod, for God had warned them in a dream to go home another way.
Matthew 2:11-12

Think

1. Why did the wise men follow the star? 2. Why did they bring special gifts for Jesus? 3. Are there some people who show that you are special to them by giving you gifts? Who are they? 4. God gave us His Son, Jesus, to show us that we are special to Him. Have you given a special gift to God?

Learn

From this story we learn that people give us special gifts when we are special people to them.

Do

Who are your three most special people? What will you give each one today?

JESUS VISITS GOD'S HOUSE

Like Jesus: OBEYING

J esus was twelve now, old enough to go to the Passover as a young man. All the people in the land went to the Passover each year, but it was special to become twelve. That's when a boy became a man.

The Passover was a time for families and friends to get together. People talked and told stories, and then ate.

Jesus traveled to the Passover with Mary and Joseph as He usually did. He did many things on His own. When the Passover was over, all the families headed home in big caravans.

Somehow Mary and Joseph thought Jesus was with some relatives. But he wasn't. They were two days away from the city when they realized that Jesus was not there.

Quickly Mary and Joseph hurried back to Jerusalem. They looked and looked. At last they found Jesus sitting in God's house, the Temple, asking the teachers many questions about God.

"Where have you been?" Mary asked. "We have been worried about you."

"Didn't you know that I would be here?" Jesus asked.

But now when it was time to go home, Jesus left the teachers in God's house. He stopped asking important questions. And He went home with Joseph and Mary.

Jesus was a big boy now. He was old enough to behave like a man. But we are told that He obeyed Mary and Joseph, just as He always did.

If Jesus obeyed, don't you think it's a good idea for you too?

He was in the Temple, sitting among the teachers of the Law, discussing deep questions with them. Luke 2:46

Think

1. Why did Jesus get to do more things when He became twelve?
2. What did He do at God's house? 3. What did He do when Mary and Joseph came looking for Him? 4. Why should you obey your parents?

Learn

From this story we learn that Jesus obeyed His parents.

Do

Make a yellow smiling face and a blue frowning face. When you obey, hang up the smiling face. When you don't obey, hang up the frowning face.

JESUS IS BAPTIZED

Like Jesus: DOING SOMETHING FIRST

I f you saw John the Baptist, walking down your street, you would think he looked strange. He was a desert man, with clothes made from camels' hair. John did not eat what you eat either. He often ate locusts, something like grasshoppers, and wild honey.

But John was quite a preacher. People came from everywhere to hear him. They knew that John spent much time alone with God. John had some important things to say.

One day a crowd gathered around John near the Jordan River. There were rich people and poor people, tax collectors and soldiers. It seemed that everyone had come to hear what John was going to say.

"You must be sorry for your sins," John preached to the people. "You must obey God and do what you know is right."

The people listened. Some believed what John said, that God could save them from their sins and would help them do what was right. When they asked God to forgive them, John baptized them in the river.

But John was angry at some of the people who wanted to be baptized. "You say you love God, but you don't show it in your lives," John told them. "Just because you are baptized doesn't mean that God will forgive your sins."

"What should we do then?" the people asked.

"Do you have an extra coat?" John asked. "Give it to someone who has none. Always tell the truth, even if you will be punished for doing so. And don't always wish you had something your friends have. Be happy with what you have."

Many of the people did what John told them. They were amazed at how much John knew about God. "Everyone is saying that the Messiah, the Savior of Israel, is coming soon," someone told John. "Are you this great King?"

John shook his head. "No, I am not the one," he told them. "When I baptize you, it is only with water. But when this Messiah comes, He will baptize you with the Spirit of God. He is so great that I am not even good enough to untie His sandals. He is God's Son. You will see Him soon. But when He comes, you will see more and more of Him and less and less of me. That is the way it should be."

The next day John saw Jesus walking along the road by the river. "There He is," John said. "He is the Lamb of God. He will

"With water I baptize those who repent of their sins; but someone else is coming, far greater than I am, so great that I am not worthy to carry His shoes! He shall baptize you with the Holy Spirit and with fire." Matthew 3:11

This Egyptian locust, one of many members of the grasshopper family, looks like the Bible-time locust that John the Baptist ate. John's diet is still common in certain Muslim countries, where the poor depend on locusts for protein. Some people preserve locusts by drying them and crushing them into powder for flour. John received sugar from wild honey and protein from locusts.

take away the sins of the world. He is the one I was talking about when I said I am not good enough to untie His sandals."

Jesus walked down the river bank to the water's edge. "I want you to baptize Me, John," He said.

John did not want to do it. "You should be baptizing me," he told Jesus. "You are God's Son, and my job is to point others to You."

But Jesus insisted. "God wants you to do this," He said. Jesus would do first what He asked others to do. If He would ask others to be baptized, He wanted to be baptized first. So John baptized Jesus in the Jordan River.

As Jesus came up out of the water, John looked up and saw the heavens open and the Spirit of God come down on Jesus like a dove. A voice spoke from heaven at the same time. It was God's voice.

"This is My Son, whom I love very much," God said. "Listen to Him!"

From this day on, John was sure that Jesus was God's Son. He knew that the promised Messiah had come at last. John must have been glad, too, that God's Son wanted to be baptized first before He asked others to be baptized.

This is the One I was talking about when I said, "Someone is coming who is greater by far than I am...." For Moses gave us only the Law with its rigid demands and merciless justice, while Jesus Christ brought us loving forgiveness as well.
John 1:15,17

Think

1. What did Jesus want John to do to Him? 2. Why did Jesus ask John to do this? 3. Are you glad when someone does something first, before asking you to do it? Why?

Learn

From this story we learn that it is good to do something first before asking others to do it.

Do

Do you ask your brother, or sister, or friend to do things you wouldn't want to do? Print the words TRY IT FIRST on a sign and hang it in your room. The sign will remind you not to ask people to do things you wouldn't do.

JESUS MEETS SATAN
Like Jesus: RESISTING TEMPTATION

After Jesus was baptized, He went into the desert to be alone with God. There He stayed for forty days and nights. And He had nothing to eat.

After all those days, when Jesus was aching for food, Satan came to see Him. He knew how terribly hungry Jesus was, so he tried to tempt Him to sin.

"If you are God's Son, why not turn these stones into bread?" Satan asked. Jesus could do it easily. Then He would have something to eat. So why not? But Jesus did not want to do things Satan's way. So He answered Satan from God's Word.

"We need more than bread to live," Jesus told Satan. "We live by obeying God and His Word."

Satan tried again to tempt Jesus to do wrong. He took Jesus to the highest point on the Temple wall in Jerusalem. "Jump! The angels will keep you from falling," Satan suggested. But Jesus would be obeying Satan, not God, and Jesus could not do that. So He answered Satan from God's Word again.

"You must not tempt the Lord, your God," Jesus said.

Satan tried one last time. He took Jesus to a high mountain and offered Him all the power and riches of the world if Jesus would only worship Satan. But Jesus spoke God's Word again.

"You must worship God only," Jesus said. "Get out of here!"

Satan left, for he saw now that he could not get Jesus to sin. Jesus had said no three times by speaking God's Word. That's a good way to say no to Satan, isn't it?

After Satan was gone, angels came to take care of Jesus. They gave Him all that He needed.

"I'll give it all to You," [Satan] said, "if You will only kneel and worship me."

"Get out of here, Satan," Jesus told him. "The Scriptures say, 'Worship only the Lord God. Obey only Him.'"

Then Satan went away, and the angels came and cared for Jesus. Matthew 4:9-11

Think

1. What was Satan trying to get Jesus to do? 2. How did Jesus say no to Satan? 3. How should you say no to Satan when he tempts you? Will you remember that?

Learn

From this story we learn that Jesus resisted Satan's temptations by using God's Word.

Do

Choose one of these two verses to memorize: 1 Corinthians 10:13, or Philippians 4:13. They will help you say no to Satan when he tempts you.

JESUS' FIRST DISCIPLES
Like Jesus: LEADING IN GOD'S WAY

Jesus was now ready to do the work God had sent Him to do. But Jesus needed some helpers.

One day Jesus walked by the Jordan River. John the Baptist said to some friends, "There is the Lamb of God, the Messiah I told you about."

Two of John's friends walked up the road to meet Jesus.

"We want to know You better," they said. "Where do You live?"

Jesus took the two men to the place where He was staying. They spent all day talking about God. Jesus told them many wonderful things. If these men were going to help Him, they must know about God and His work.

Now these men were sure that Jesus was God's Son. One ran to find his brother, Simon. "I have found the Messiah," Andrew said. Then Andrew brought Simon to Jesus. Simon also knew that he had found God's Son.

The next day Jesus met Philip. When Philip heard Jesus, he ran to bring his friend Nathaniel to see Him.

"Here is a good man," Jesus said when Nathaniel came.

"We've never met," Nathaniel said. "How do you know anything about me?"

"I saw you under the fig tree before Philip came for you," Jesus said.

"You must be God's Son," said Nathaniel. "I would like to follow you, too."

Soon Jesus had a small group of followers, or helpers. They became known as His disciples. They wanted to follow Jesus because they knew He would teach them and lead them in God's way. That is a good way to follow, isn't it?

The following day, as John was standing with two of his disciples, Jesus walked by. John looked at Him intently and then declared, "See! There is the Lamb of God!" Then John's two disciples turned and followed Jesus. John 1:35-37

Think

1. Which four men became His first helpers? 2. Why did they want to follow Jesus? 3. Why will others want to follow you or help you do God's work? What should you do?

Learn

From this story we learn that the disciples wanted to follow Jesus because He would lead them in the right way—God's way.

Do

Print the words GOD'S WAY on a paper flag and hang it over your door. It will remind you that His way is the right way each day.

JESUS GOES TO A WEDDING
Like Jesus: CONCERNED FOR OTHERS

The wedding in Cana was like other weddings of Jesus' time. But it was not like weddings today! There was no church service, and no minister to say that the bride and groom were married. The wedding ceremony was a big party! The party began when the bridegroom went to the bride's house to bring her to his house.

Of course, friends went with him and there was much excitement. While the bride waited at her house, her friends waited with her. If it got dark, they lighted their oil lamps to carry in the streets on their way to the bridegroom's house.

At the bridegroom's house his friends prepared a big dinner. All the friends and relatives stayed and ate with the bride and groom. They stayed there, not just for the afternoon, but for a week. Sometimes they even stayed for two weeks.

So, on the day of the wedding in Cana, you can see how excited the disciples were as they made their way with Jesus to the bridegroom's house. They would enjoy talking and eating with their friends for many days.

When they arrived in Cana, the town was filled with excitement. Friends and neighbors were running here and there, preparing the dinner. Mary, Jesus' mother, was helping. The bridegroom was probably a family friend.

At last the wedding was about to begin. The dinner was ready at the bridegroom's house and all the guests had arrived.

Imagine the excitement as the groom headed down the street with his friends. They must have been singing and laughing. Perhaps his friends teased the groom, too.

The guests watched with delight as the bride came from her house and joined the groom for the walk back to his house. Now there was even more singing and laughter, for all the bride's family and friends came along.

At last everyone was at the groom's house and dinner began. People talked and ate. They ate and drank. And they drank and talked some more. What a party this was!

But after a few days the man in charge of the dinner became worried. They did not have enough wine. Of course, if they ran out of wine, it would look as though he had not prepared well.

Somehow Mary heard about the man's problem. She felt sorry for the man. She also felt sorry for the bride and groom. What would they think if their wedding celebration was not right?

...Jesus' mother came to Him with the problem. "I can't help you now," He said. "It isn't yet My time for miracles." But His mother told the servants, "Do whatever He tells you to." John 2:3-5

Today most of our pots and pans
are made of metal or glass. In Jesus'
time they were made of clay, usually
shaped on a potter's wheel, and
baked until hard. Clay pots were
made in different shapes. Archae-
ologists can tell what period of
history they are uncovering by the
shapes of the pots. Some jars sat on
the floor, others on a stand, such as
this.

Mary decided she would tell Jesus about the problem. He could help.

"What can I do?" Jesus told her. "I am not supposed to do any miracles yet."

But Mary knew that Jesus was concerned about His friends. She was sure that He could help, and would help. So Mary said to the helpers at the dinner, "Do whatever Jesus tells you to do."

Jesus looked around the room where the people were eating. He saw six large water jars.

"Fill those jars with water," Jesus told the helpers at the dinner. "Then dip out a cupful and take it to the man in charge of the dinner."

The helpers were surprised. Why should they take water to the man in charge? That certainly would not make him happy. He wanted wine for the dinner.

But the helpers did exactly what Jesus said, just as Mary had told them to do. One by one they filled the giant jars with water. Then they dipped a cup into a jar and took it to the man in charge.

The man put the cup to his lips and drank. Then he called for the bridegroom to come.

"Where did you get this?" he asked. "It is the most wonderful wine I have tasted. Most people serve their best wine first, but you have saved it until last."

Jesus' disciples saw what had happened. "That was a miracle!" they said. "Now we know that Jesus is God's Son. Only God's Son could do a miracle like that."

Mary saw what happened too. She knew that Jesus helped because He cared for others. Jesus was always concerned for His friends, and ready to help them. Wouldn't you like to be like Jesus and show concern for your friends?

When the master of ceremonies tasted the water that was now wine, not knowing where it had come from (though, of course, the servants did), he called the bridegroom over.

"...You're different from most.... You have kept the best for the last!"
John 3:9,10

Think

1. What were weddings like in Jesus' time? 2. Why do you think Jesus and His friends were so happy to be there? 3. What happened that could have spoiled the wedding? 4. How did Jesus show concern?

Learn

From this story we learn that Jesus showed concern for those in need.

Do

Write the names of three people for whom you should be concerned today. How can you show them you care?

JESUS AND MONEYCHANGERS
Like Jesus: RESPECTING GOD'S HOUSE

Each year people came from all over the land to the Passover feast in Jerusalem. Jesus and His disciples came too.

But when they came to worship at God's house, the Temple, Jesus became angry. Instead of a quiet place where people could pray, God's house had become a noisy marketplace. People were selling sheep, cows and doves in the courtyard. Moneychangers piled their tables high with money. People were shouting and trying to make deals.

"This is not right," Jesus said to His disciples. "We must have reverence [show respect] for God's house. These people are not treating God's house the way it should be treated."

Jesus made some strands of rope into a whip. He chased the merchants away with this whip. He turned over the tables of money and drove out the cows and sheep.

"Take all this away," Jesus commanded. "God's house is a place to pray and worship. It is not a place to buy and sell animals."

Of course the moneychangers were angry at Jesus. "Who gave you the right to do this?" they demanded. "Who are you?"

Jesus could have told them who He was. But they would not have believed Him. He could have told them that He was God's Son, but they would have laughed at Him.

Instead, Jesus went into God's house to worship. That's why He came there in the first place. Don't you think He was right to show such reverence for God's house? Don't you want to show that reverence for God's house, too?

Jesus...drove out the sheep and oxen, scattering the moneychangers' coins over the floor and turning over their tables! Then, going over to the men selling doves, He told them, "Get these things out of here. Don't turn My Father's House into a market!"
John 2:15-16

Think

1. Why did Jesus go to God's house? What did He want to do?
2. Why was He angry when He arrived? 3. What did He do to show reverence for God's house? 4. What are some ways you can show reverence for God's house?

John 2:13-25

Learn

From this story we learn that Jesus showed reverence for God's house and that we should also.

Do

Ask your pastor or Sunday school teacher to help you make a list of four ways you and your friends can show reverence for God's house.

NICODEMUS

Like Jesus: SHOWING THE WAY TO GOD

The streets of Jerusalem were filled with people. They had come from all over the land to spend the week at the great Passover feast. Each year people came, and the city overflowed with crowds.

Little groups of people sat and talked. They ate together and talked about their families and friends. People loved to come for this great feast, for it was like a big family reunion.

But Jesus did not sit around talking that way. He wanted to teach and preach to all these people. He wanted to heal the sick and help people know about God.

When each day ended, Jesus went to the house of a friend. Often He would sit on the rooftop to pray and think.

One night Jesus was sitting on this rooftop. Below Him the muffled noises of the city could be heard everywhere. But as Jesus looked up at the stars and felt the soft wind blowing, He felt close to God.

Suddenly there was a knock at the door of the house and the owner brought a man to the rooftop where Jesus sat. This visitor was an important man, one of the great teachers in Jerusalem. But tonight he had not come to teach Jesus, he had come to listen to Jesus.

"We know that God has sent you to teach us," Nicodemus said to Jesus. "The great miracles you do prove that you are from God."

Jesus looked closely at His guest. He knew that Nicodemus had not come just to say that. Jesus knew that Nicodemus had come to ask about his own relationship to God.

"If you want to live with God in heaven, you must be born again," Jesus told Nicodemus. The man was startled. Jesus had answered his question before he had asked it.

"Born again? How can an old man like me go back into his mother and be born again?" Nicodemus asked.

"You were born once from your mother," Jesus said. "But you need to be born again into God's family by His Spirit."

Nicodemus looked puzzled. Never before had he heard such a thing.

"But how does this happen?" he asked.

"Are you a great teacher and you do not know this?" Jesus asked. "I am teaching you things that I have seen, so won't you believe me? What if I teach you things about heaven, where I, God's Son, once lived and where I shall return?"

After dark one night a Jewish religious leader named Nicodemus, a member of the sect of the Pharisees, came for an interview with Jesus. John 3:1

Nicodemus was a religious leader of
the Jewish people of Jesus' time.
He knew God's Word thoroughly
and wrote on scrolls like this one
studied by modern Jewish students.
Scrolls were made of papyrus (paper
made from reedy plants), leather,
or parchment (paper made from
animal skins) wound on wooden
rollers. They were about a foot in
height and no more than 30 feet
long. In early scrolls, writing went
from right to left. Scrolls were the
books of Jesus' time.

Nicodemus listened quietly. This is what he had come to hear.

"For God loved everyone in this world so much that He sent Me, His only Son, to save every person who believes in Him," Jesus told Nicodemus. "Those who do not believe that I am God's Son will keep on sinning, and will one day be severely punished."

Nicodemus had never heard a teacher like Jesus before. He and his friends had taught people rules about what to do and what not to do. Most of their rules were about things that people should not do. But Jesus talked about God's home in heaven and how to get there. He taught about starting a new life by being born again into God's family.

We do not know when Nicodemus received Jesus and became a Christian, but he did. Later, when Jesus was crucified, it was Nicodemus who brought spices to put on His body.

Perhaps it was that night after Jesus and he talked on the rooftop that Nicodemus was born into God's family!

For God loved the world so much that He gave His only Son so that anyone who believes in Him shall not perish but have eternal life. God did not send His Son into the world to condemn it, but to save it. John 3:16-17

Think

1. Who was Nicodemus? What did he do? 2. Why did Nicodemus come to see Jesus? 3. What did Jesus tell him? Why was this so important for Nicodemus to know?

Learn

From this story we learn that Jesus showed others the way to God. He even told a great teacher how to be born again into God's family. We should tell others, too.

Do

Have you ever accepted Jesus as your Savior? If not, ask someone who knows about it to help you do that now.

THE WOMAN AT THE WELL
Like Jesus: SHOWING THE WAY TO GOD

ne day Jesus and His disciples were walking through the area of Samaria. About lunchtime they stopped near the town of Sychar and rested by a well. Jacob had dug this well long ago and given it to his son Joseph.

The disciples were hungry and wanted to eat lunch. "We will go into town and buy some food," they said to Jesus.

Jesus was tired from the long walk in the hot sun. So He sat alone next to the well and waited for the disciples to return.

Before long a Samaritan woman came from town, carrying a large water jug on her head. She stopped by the well to get water to fill her jug.

"May I have a drink of water?" Jesus asked.

The woman was surprised as she looked at Jesus. Most Jewish men did not talk to Samaritan women.

"Why is it that you are asking me for water?" she said.

"If you knew who I am," Jesus told her, "you would ask Me for living water." The woman was puzzled.

"How will you get this living water?" she asked. "You don't even have a rope or bucket to get it up from the well."

Jesus pointed to the woman's water jug. "When you drink that water, you will become thirsty again," He told her. "But when you drink My living water, you will always be satisfied."

"Please tell me where I can find this living water," the woman begged. "Then I will never have to make this long walk to this well again."

The woman did not understand that Jesus was talking about Himself. So He tried to help her see who He really was.

"Find your husband," Jesus told her. "I would like to talk with him, too."

"But I don't have a husband," she said.

"You are right," Jesus told her. "You have had five husbands and you are not married to the man you now live with."

"You must be some kind of prophet," the woman said. "How did you know all that?"

"I am more than prophet," Jesus told her. "The time has come when the Messiah will offer eternal life to anyone who believes in Him. Where you worship is no longer important. But how you worship is important. We are to read God's Word and ask His Holy Spirit to help us understand it and to worship Him as we should."

[Jesus] replied, "If you only knew what a wonderful gift God has for you, and who I am, you would ask Me for some living water!"
John 4:10

In Bible lands today, churches are
built over many of the places where
Bible events happened. Several
churches have been built over Jacob's
well through the years. The church
over Jacob's well today is not
completed. The well is 75 feet deep
today and was probably much deeper
in Jesus' time. It was dug on land
that Jacob gave to his son, Joseph.

"This Messiah you mentioned," said the woman. "I know that He is God's Son, and I know that He is coming soon. When He comes, He will explain all this to us."

"The Messiah has already come," Jesus told her. "I am the living water I told you about."

Just then the disciples returned from town with the food. They were surprised to see Jesus talking with a Samaritan. They were even more surprised when they found out the sinful things this woman had done.

The woman left her water jug by the well and ran into town to tell her friends about who she had met. "Come and meet this man," she said to her friends. "He told me all that I have done. Can He be the Messiah, God's Son?"

Jesus and His disciples looked toward the city gate. Crowds of people were streaming out of the city gate to see Jesus.

"Look!" Jesus told His disciples. "People all around you are searching for God. We need people who will show them the way."

Many of the Samaritans believed that Jesus was God's Son because of the things the woman told them. Others begged Him to stay and talk with them.

So Jesus stayed in Samaria two days, telling these people about the way to God. Many more of them believed because of the things He said.

"Now we believe because of the things we have heard from Jesus ourselves," the Samaritans said. "He is truly the Savior, the way to God."

Then the woman left her waterpot beside the well and went back to the village and told everyone, "Come and meet a man who told me everything I ever did! Can this be the Messiah?" So the people came streaming from the village to see Him. John 4:28-30

Think

1. Why did the Samaritan woman believe that Jesus could be the Son of God? 2. Why did Jesus describe Himself as the living water? 3. Why did some believe at first? 4. Why did more believe later?

Learn

From this story we learn that Jesus showed people the way to God. We should do that also.

Do

Have you been born into God's family? If not, ask someone who knows about it to help you pray and receive Jesus now as your Savior. Think of one friend who does not know Jesus. Would you like to help this person know the way to God through Jesus? Why not talk to this friend today?

A BIG CATCH OF FISH

Like Jesus: HELPING THOSE WHO NEED US

Peter, Andrew, James and John were partners in a small fishing business on the Sea of Galilee. One day, after supper, they piled their nets into their two fishing boats and sailed out onto the water.

As the evening wore on, they threw out their big nets and pulled them to the boat again. But the nets were empty. There were no fish in them. They tried again, but still they caught nothing. Again and again the disciples of Jesus threw their nets into the water, first on one side of the boat, and then on the other. All night they tried, but they did not catch a single fish.

When morning came, the fishermen gave up and headed their boats back to shore. You know how discouraged they must have been as they sat on the beach, cleaning and mending their nets.

As they talked about the long tiring night, they looked up and saw Jesus coming toward them. A large crowd followed Him, listening to Him tell about God and His home in heaven.

Jesus stopped by the water's edge and began to speak. But so many people crowded around Him that He could not speak to them all.

Then Jesus saw Peter. "Will you please push your boat into the water?" Jesus asked. Then Jesus sat in Peter's boat and talked to the people from there. Now everyone could see Jesus and hear Him speak. After He had taught them for some time, the people went home.

When everyone had left, Jesus turned toward Peter, who was sitting there with Him. "Let's go fishing," Jesus told Peter.

"Sir, we have already fished all night," Peter answered Jesus. "We did not catch a single fish. But if You think we should try again, we will."

Jesus pointed to one place where He wanted them to go. So Peter and Andrew rowed there. Once again they threw their net into the water.

"Pull!" Peter shouted.

The two grabbed the corner of the net and began to pull. But something was different now. It was hard to pull the net toward the boat.

"Look!" Andrew cried out. "The net is filled with fish. I have never seen so many!"

Peter could hardly believe what he saw. The net was so full of fish that it began to tear.

"Hurry! Come and help us!" Peter shouted to James and John

who were still on the beach.

Quickly James and John brought their boat out. Together they pulled the big net into Peter's boat. But there were so many fish that the boat began to sink. So they put half the fish into the boat James and John were using. Even then their boat almost sank.

As the fishermen made their way toward shore and the excitement died down, Peter stared at Jesus. He thought about the long night of fishing when they had caught nothing. He realized that Jesus had taken them to this great school of fish and helped them catch more fish than they had ever caught before.

How did Jesus do this? No ordinary man could ever know exactly where those fish were.

When the boats reached shore, Peter jumped out and fell on the ground at Jesus' feet. He was afraid, for he realized again who Jesus was, that He was surely God's Son.

"Please leave us," Peter begged. "I am a sinner and you should not even be around us."

Peter asked Jesus to leave because he thought that God's Son was too great to be with ordinary sinful people.

Jesus smiled. "Peter, I helped you catch fish today, but now I will help you catch men for God," he said.

Peter could not understand what Jesus was saying. But someday he would realize that Jesus could help him bring people to God as easily as He had helped Peter catch fish. Jesus can help us any time we need Him.

The next time we need someone to help us, we should remember what Jesus can do. Jesus will help when we truly need Him. The next time a friend or family member needs us to help them, we should be ready to help, just like Jesus helped the disciples.

Peter, Andrew, James and John were fishermen on the Sea of Galilee. Their fishing partner was Zebedee, father of James and John. When the four became Jesus' disciples, Zebedee continued the fishing business. James and John, of course, gave up their inheritance to be Jesus' disciples. The Sea of Galilee is an inland lake about 60 miles north of Jerusalem. It is about 150 feet deep.

Think

1. How did Jesus help the fishermen? What did He help them do? 2. How do you think Jesus can help us bring people to God? 3. Why should you be ready to help friends and family members when they need you?

For [Peter] was awestruck by the size of their catch, as were the others with him, and his partners too— James and John, the sons of Zebedee. Jesus replied, "Don't be afraid! From now on you'll be fishing for the souls of men!" Luke 5:9-10

Learn

From this story we learn that Jesus is ready to help us when we truly need Him. We should be ready to help others when they need us, too.

Do

Ask your mother or father how you can help them most today. Then do it.

MATTHEW FOLLOWS JESUS
Like Jesus: HELPING THOSE WHO NEED US

When Jesus was on earth, the Romans ruled the land where He lived. The Jewish people hated their Roman rulers. They especially hated the tax collectors. Sometimes these were Jews who worked for the Romans, forcing their own people to pay taxes to the Romans.

Matthew, whose name at first was Levi, was one of those hated tax collectors. He worked at a booth along the road to Jesus' adopted home town, Capernaum.

Jesus often stopped to talk to Matthew. He must have asked Matthew often to follow God's ways and stop what he was doing. But Matthew did not. Then one day Jesus walked up to Matthew's booth again.

What was different about that day? We don't know. But this time when Jesus said to Matthew, "Follow Me!" Matthew closed up his tax booth and went to work with Jesus.

Soon after that, Matthew invited Jesus to supper at his house. Matthew's friends were there, friends the neighbors did not like, for several of his friends were tax collectors too.

Some grumpy men did not like Jesus eating with Matthew and his friends. They complained to Jesus' disciples.

"Why does Jesus eat with people like that?" they demanded to know.

Jesus heard them. "People who are well do not need a doctor," Jesus told them. "People need a doctor when they are sick. I have come to help sinners turn from their sins, not to spend time with those who think they are already good enough."

Jesus was saying that He wanted to help those who really needed Him. Perhaps that is what we should do, too.

Think

1. Why did many people not like Matthew? 2. How did Jesus treat Matthew? What did He ask Matthew to do? 3. What did Matthew do? 4. Why were some grumpy men angry at Jesus? What did they say? How did Jesus answer them? Why should we help those who really need us?

Jesus...saw a tax collector—with the usual reputation for cheating—sitting at a tax collection booth. The man's name was Levi. Jesus said to him, "Come and be one of My disciples!" Luke 5:27

Learn

From this story we learn that Jesus helped those who really needed Him.

Do

Who really needs your help today? Think of something Jesus would do, that you could do too, that would help that person, and then do it.

HEALING BY THE POOL
Like Jesus: SHOWING COMPASSION

Crowds of people made their way to Jerusalem again for one of the great feasts held there. Jesus and His disciples traveled to Jerusalem too.

When they arrived in Jerusalem, they entered the city through a large gate. Nearby was a pool, called Bethesda, with five porches surrounding it.

Jesus stopped. Large groups of people lay on these porches. Each person stayed as close to the water as possible.

The disciples noticed that all of these people were crippled, or sick, or blind. One of them was a man who had been lying on a mat for thirty-eight years. He could not walk.

These people were waiting for the water to stir. They had heard that an angel came from time to time to stir the water. The first person to get into the water after that would be healed.

Jesus spoke to the man who had been lying there for all those years. "Would you like to get well?" Jesus asked Him.

"Of course," the man said. "But how can I? There is no one to take me into the water when it stirs. Someone always gets there ahead of me."

Jesus looked at the man with compassion.

"Get up!" Jesus told the man. "Roll up your mat and walk!"

At once the man stood up. He rolled up his mat and began walking around the pool. You can imagine how happy that man was after lying around for thirty-eight years. At last he could walk!

But some grumpy men called Pharisees were not happy about this. They had made a great many rules for the people to obey. One rule said that people could not work on the Sabbath, and that it was work to heal someone. They even had a rule that said it was wrong to carry a mat on the Sabbath day.

So when these Pharisees saw the man carrying his mat, they stopped him. They did not care that he had been sick for thirty-eight years and had just been healed. It was more important to them that he was breaking a rule.

"Don't you know it is wrong to carry your mat on the Sabbath?" they demanded.

"But the man who healed me told me to," he answered.

"Who? Who told you to do this?" they wanted to know.

But the man did not know who Jesus was. And by this time Jesus had disappeared in the crowd.

Inside the city, near the Sheep Gate, was Bethesda Pool, with platforms or porches surrounding it. Crowds of sick folks — lame, blind, or with paralyzed limbs — lay on the platforms (waiting for a certain movement of the water...)
John 5:2,3

In this picture we are looking down into the Pool of Bethesda and the ruins of the porches around it. The pool is located in the area near the Dome of the Rock (a Muslim mosque on the site of the ancient Temple) today. Through the years the area has been filled in with dirt and stones from destroyed buildings. The ground level today is about a story (15-20 feet) higher than it was in Jesus' time.

Later the man saw Jesus in the Temple. "You are well now," Jesus told the man. So now the man knew who Jesus was.

These grumpy Pharisees complained to Jesus that He was breaking their rules. They did not have compassion for this man as Jesus did.

Jesus showed that He cared for those who hurt. It was more important to Him to heal a person than to keep those grumpy men's many rules. Jesus cares when others hurt. Don't you think that's a good idea for you too?

Think

1. Who healed the man who had been sick for thirty-eight years?
2. Which was more important for Jesus, to heal the man or to obey one of the Pharisees' unnecessary rules? Why? 3. Why should you show that you care about others who hurt?

One of the men lying there had been sick for thirty-eight years. When Jesus saw him and knew how long he had been ill, He asked him, "Would you like to get well?" John 5:5,6

So the Jewish leaders objected. "You can't work on the Sabbath! It's illegal to carry that sleeping mat!" John 5:10,11

Learn

From this story we learn that Jesus thought it was more important to show compassion to someone who hurt than to obey a useless rule.

Do

Look up the word COMPASSION in the dictionary. What does it mean? How can you show compassion to someone?

JESUS CHOOSES TWELVE

Like Jesus: MAKING RIGHT CHOICES

Have you ever heard someone tell a story so wonderful that you did not want him to stop? Jesus told stories like that.

People traveled for miles to listen to Jesus. He talked about things they had never heard before, such as forgiveness of sins and a life in heaven that never ends.

"We have never heard a man speak like this," people said. "Jesus is no ordinary man. He is different."

Of course Jesus was different. He was God's Son. Soon many believed in Him. Some people wanted to be with Jesus wherever He went. They wanted to hear everything He said and find out what these things meant.

These loyal men and women were Jesus' followers. One day He asked them to walk with Him to a quiet hillside. There He chose twelve men to be His disciples, those with whom He would work most closely.

Each of these disciples would have an important part in helping Jesus do the work God had sent Him to do. Jesus told them many things about God that He never told anyone else. He knew that He must train these men to say what God wanted them to say and to do what God wanted them to do. When they were trained, He would send them out to do God's work.

In the stories that follow you will see many wonderful things that these disciples saw and learn many wonderful lessons they learned.

Jesus was glad God helped Him choose the right men to be His disciples. When you must choose something important, don't you think you should ask God to help you, too?

At daybreak He called together His followers and chose twelve of them to be the inner circle of His disciples. Luke 6:13

Think

1. Why did people come to hear Jesus? 2. How many did He choose as His special helpers? What were they to do for Him? 3. Who can help you choose the right way?

Mark 3:13-19

Learn

From this story we learn that Jesus made the right choices in helpers. We want to make right choices too, and God can help us do that.

Do

Write two words, CHOOSE—PRAY on a card and hang it over your door. It will remind you to pray before you make any choice today.

JESUS' SERMON ON A MOUNT
Like Jesus: TELLING THE GOOD NEWS

One day a crowd began to gather around Jesus. This was not unusual, for crowds gathered around Him wherever He went.

Jesus told His followers to come with Him. Then He climbed up a high hill. When they reached the top, Jesus sat down and began to teach them.

"Do you want to know how to be happy?" Jesus asked. Then Jesus told them some ways to be happy. Here are some of those ways.

"People who want to do right and be good are happy," Jesus said. "So are those who are kind and merciful, and those whose hearts are pure. Happy are those who want peace and work to get it. Even those who are treated wrong because they try to do right are happy."

Jesus taught His followers for a long time. He taught them how to be happy by sharing the Good News of why He had come into the world. He told them He had come to die to pay for their sins. Of course Jesus was happy because He was doing what God wanted Him to do. He was sharing the Good News of why He had come, with people wherever He went.

Jesus finished His teaching by telling the people, "Whoever listens to what I teach and does what I say is wise, but whoever listens and does not do what I teach is foolish."

The people were surprised when they listened to Jesus teach. They had heard many teachers, but this was the first time they had heard a teacher talk about being happy.

Jesus was telling them the Good News about why He had come. And He knew what He was talking about!

"Humble men are very fortunate!" He told them, "for the Kingdom of Heaven is given to them. Those who mourn are fortunate! for they shall be comforted. The meek and lowly are fortunate! for the whole wide world belongs to them." Matthew 5:3-5

Think

1. What did Jesus teach? 2. Why did He know so much about God? 3. Why did He want to tell the Good News? 4. Why should you tell the Good News?

Learn

From this story we learn that Jesus taught people the Good News about God. That's good for us to do too.

Do

Read the following verses that tell about Good News or Glad Tidings of Jesus: Luke 2:10, 11; Luke 8:1; John 3:16. What is the Good News?

RAISING A WIDOW'S SON
Like Jesus: HELPING PEOPLE WHO HURT

People were crowding around Jesus as He went into the village of Nain. They hoped He would help them or teach them about God.

Suddenly the people stopped and became very quiet. Up ahead, coming out of the village was a line of people. They were crying and moaning.

"It's a funeral," someone must have whispered.

Leading the procession were some men carrying an open coffin. And in that coffin was a young man who had died. He was wrapped in burial clothes.

Behind the coffin walked the young man's mother. Her husband had already died, and now her only son was dead also. There was no one left to take care of her.

Jesus saw the poor woman crying and felt sorry for her. He knew how much she was hurting.

"Please don't cry," Jesus said to the woman.

Then Jesus walked over to the coffin and touched it. "Son, come back to life again!" Jesus said to the young man.

The young man sat up in the coffin. You can imagine how that mother must have felt! Don't you think she ran up to her son and hugged him and kissed him?

Of course the people were quite amazed to see what had happened. Many of them were afraid, for they had never seen a dead man come back to life.

"He must be a great prophet," the people said. "We have seen God work today!"

The people had seen Jesus help a woman who was hurting. Shouldn't we ask Jesus to show us how we can help those who hurt too?

He walked over to the coffin and touched it, and the bearers stopped. "Laddie," He said, "come back to life again." Then the boy sat up and began to talk. Luke 7:14,15

Think

1. How did Jesus help this woman who was hurting? 2. Why do you think He did this? 3. How can you help someone who is hurting? Will you?

Learn

From this story we learn that Jesus helped people who were hurting. We should too.

Do

Which of these events cause people to hurt? A cut finger, a friend who died, a pet that died, a father who lost his job, an unkind word. Can you name others?

ALL ABOUT SEEDS
Like Jesus: HELPING OTHERS TO KNOW

Jesus loved to tell stories. People followed Him everywhere to listen to them.

One day Jesus walked by the Sea of Galilee. He stepped into a boat and pushed it into the water. As the people came near to listen, Jesus told them this story about a farmer and his seeds.

A farmer went out to his field to plant seeds. As he walked back and forth, he reached into his bag for a handful of seeds and then threw them toward the ground. Some seeds were caught up by the wind and fell along the hard path next to the field. Soon birds came and ate those seeds.

Other seeds fell on stony ground. In a few days little plants sprang up. But the soil was shallow and they could not grow roots. Soon the hot sun dried up the plants.

Other seeds fell among the weeds. As the little plants started to grow, the tall weeds choked them out and they died away. But some seeds fell on good ground. The soil was rich and deep, so the birds could not find these seeds. The plants grew tall and straight. Later they produced their own seeds, which the man harvested and fed to his family.

When Jesus finished His story, the people went back to their homes. But the disciples asked Jesus, "Why do you talk in stories.

"People who want to know more about God will try to know the meaning of My stories," Jesus told them. Then Jesus explained that the seed was the Word of God. People with hard hearts are like the hard path. Others have hearts like stony ground. Others let too many things (like television, for example) choke out the Word of God. But some people let God's Word grow in their lives and it does good things.

Think

1. How was Jesus helping others understand God's Word?
2. What did Jesus say the seed was like? 3. How was the different kind of ground like people? 4. Do you like to help others understand God's Word?

"...The good ground represents the heart of a man who listens to the message and understands it and goes out and brings thirty, sixty, or even a hundred others into the Kingdom."
Matthew 13:23

Learn

From this story we learn that Jesus helped others understand God's Word.

Do

Read Acts 8:26-40 for another story about a man who helped someone understand God's Word.

JESUS QUIETS A STORM

Like Jesus: HELPING PEOPLE IN TROUBLE

I t had been a busy day for Jesus. Since morning He had been healing the sick and teaching the Good News about God by the Sea of Galilee. All day crowds followed Jesus wherever He went. But now it was time to rest.

Leaving the crowds behind, Jesus and His friends got into a boat and headed toward the other side of the Sea of Galilee. While His friends rowed the boat, He lay down to take a nap. Somewhere out on the water a storm arose. It became worse with each moment.

The waves rose up higher and higher as the wind howled across the sea. The little boat was tossed to and fro! Water splashed into the boat until it seemed that it would sink.

While all this was going on, Jesus was in the back of the boat, sound asleep. The disciples were terrified.

"Jesus! Don't you care that we are about to drown?" they cried out to Him.

Jesus woke up and turned toward the angry sea. "Be quiet!" He commanded to the wind and the waves. At once the storm went away. The wind was gone and the water became calm.

The disciples gasped when they saw what Jesus had done. "Who is this man?" they asked. "Even the wind and the waves obey Him."

As the little boat sailed on, each disciple must have thought about the mighty miracle he had seen. Just when they were in trouble, they had cried out to Jesus and He had helped them. That's something to remember when we are in trouble, isn't it? And we should also remember to help others when they cry out to us in their trouble.

Then He rebuked the wind and said to the sea, "Quiet down!" And the wind fell and there was a great calm! Mark 4:39

Think

1. How were the disciples in trouble? 2. How did Jesus help them? 3. Why do you think He liked to help people in trouble? 4. Why should you want to help people in trouble?

Learn

From this story we learn that Jesus helped people in trouble. We should do that, too.

Do

Think of one friend in trouble. Will you pray for that friend today?

JESUS FEEDS 5000
Like Jesus: SHARING FOOD

ne day Jesus went into the hills to be alone. But it was hard for Jesus to be alone these days. Everyone wanted to crowd around Him. That's because He healed many people, raised some from the dead, and did many wonderful miracles.

Before long, crowds were gathering, waiting for Jesus. When Jesus came from the hills, the people were there. Some were sick, others were blind. Some were lonely, and some eager to hear more about God.

Jesus felt sorry for all these people. They reminded Him of sheep that had no shepherd to guide them. So Jesus stayed through the after-noon, helping and teaching all these people.

But late that afternoon, the disciples became uneasy about these people. They had been there for a long time but had nothing to eat. What could they do?

"It is past suppertime," the disciples told Jesus. "Let's send these people away so they can eat. It is getting late and there is nothing to give them here."

"Why don't you feed them?" Jesus said to His disciples.

The disciples were surprised. "How can we feed them?" they asked. "It would cost a fortune to buy enough food to give to all these people."

Jesus looked at all the people. There were a lot of them, over five thousand. Jesus knew how hungry these people must be by this time. It would take a lot of food to feed them.

"Go walk through the crowds," Jesus told His disciples. "See if anyone has some food they could share with us."

So the disciples walked through the crowd looking for food. At last they returned to Jesus. A small boy was with them.

"This boy has a little basket of food," they said to Jesus. "It is the only food we could find."

"But it is only five pieces of bread and two fish," Peter answered. "It is enough for the boy. But what good will that do for five thousand people?"

"Tell the people to sit down in groups of fifty," Jesus said to the disciples.

Of course, Jesus thanked the boy for sharing his basket of food. Then Jesus took the fish and the bread in His hands and looked up toward the sky. Jesus thanked God for helping Him give all those people food to eat.

Then Andrew, Simon Peter's brother, spoke up. "There's a youngster here with five barley loaves and a couple of fish! But what good is that with all this mob?" John 6:8-9

At a place called Tabgha today, just a
short distance from Capernaum, is an
old church building. It is built over a
very old floor with mosaics (pictures
made of different colored stones or
tiles). One mosaic, shown here,
pictures a basket of bread and two
fish, recalling the feeding of the
5000. Although nobody knows for
sure, many people think Jesus fed
the 5000 at Tabgha.

Jesus began to break pieces from the fish and the bread. Again and again He reached into the basket and pulled out some more pieces of bread and fish.

Jesus gave these pieces of bread and fish to the disciples. Then the disciples took this food out among the people.

You can imagine the surprise when the disciples saw Jesus do this. They knew there were only five pieces of bread and two fish in the basket. But now they saw Jesus feeding five thousand people with nothing but that bread and fish.

"How does He do it?" they must have wondered.

"It is a miracle," said some others. "Jesus must be God's Son. Only He could do something like this."

At last everyone in the crowd had all they could eat. Then Jesus asked the disciples to collect all the leftovers. When they did, they came back to Jesus at last with twelve large baskets of food.

The people in the crowd were whispering by now. They could see what a great miracle had happened. And they knew that Jesus had done it.

"It is a miracle," they said. "He must be the great Prophet that we are expecting. Let's make Him our king!"

Jesus could see that the people were going to force Him to become king. Of course He did not want to be a king. He had come to do God's work.

So Jesus slipped away alone while His disciples got into their boat and headed home. Jesus did not want to rule that crowd. He only wanted to feed them and show them God's love. Shouldn't we be like Jesus, showing love to those who are hungry?

Breaking the loaves into pieces, He gave some of the bread and fish to each disciple to place before the people. Mark 6:41

Think

1. Why were these people out there with Jesus? 2. Why did they get hungry? 3. How did Jesus feed them? 4. Why should we help to feed hungry people?

Learn

From this story we learn that Jesus was concerned that people were hungry. He loved them so much he provided food for everyone.

Do

Is there someone in your town who needs a basket of food? Could you and some friends get a basket for these people? Ask mother or father to help you be like Jesus in sharing love to those who are hungry.

JESUS WALKS ON WATER

Like Jesus: HELPING PEOPLE IN TROUBLE

fter Jesus fed 5000 people, He went up into the hills to be alone. The disciples got into their boat and headed home toward Capernaum.

You can imagine the talk on the way home. They had seen Jesus take a boy's lunch and feed all those people with it. What a miracle!

The disciples were so busy talking that they hardly noticed the wind blowing harder and harder. Suddenly they realized that they were rowing as hard as they could but were going nowhere.

Jesus saw this too, and began to go toward their boat...walking across the water! As Jesus came near the boat, it looked as if He would walk past them.

The disciples thought He was a ghost, and they screamed in terror. But Jesus spoke to them.

"Don't be afraid," He said. Then He told them who He was.

Peter leaned over the side of the boat. "Jesus, is that You?" he shouted. "If it is, let me walk to You on the water."

"Come on," Jesus told him.

Peter took one step, then another. He was walking on the water! But then Peter took his eyes off Jesus. He looked at the water. Then he began to sink.

"Help me, Jesus!" Peter cried out. So Jesus reached out His hand and helped Peter into the boat.

Jesus got into the boat too, and immediately the wind and the waves died down. Jesus helped the disciples, and Peter, when they were in trouble. Jesus is always there to help when we are in trouble. Wouldn't you like to be that way with others?

"All right," the Lord said, "come along!"

So Peter went over the side of the boat and walked on the water toward Jesus. Matthew 14:29

Think

1. How did Peter and the other disciples get into trouble? 2. Who came to help them? 3. Why do you think Jesus wants to help us when we get into trouble? 4. Why should you want to help others in trouble?

Learn

From this story we learn that Jesus will help us in times of trouble. That's good for us to do for others, too.

Do

When was the last time you saw a friend in trouble? What did you do? Talk about this with mother or father.

THE BREAD OF LIFE
Like Jesus: SHARING GOD'S GIFT

J esus had performed two great miracles in one evening. He had fed 5000 people with only a small basket of food and then had walked across the stormy sea to help His struggling disciples.

The next morning, the crowd that Jesus had fed was still looking for Him. They didn't know, of course, that He had walked across the water.

"Where did Jesus go?" the people asked one another. At last they realized that Jesus was not there, so they got into their own boats and headed for home. When they reached Capernaum they saw Jesus was there already, walking toward the synagogue.

"How did you get over here?" they asked Him.

"Are you looking for Me because you want to believe in Me?" Jesus asked. "Or are you looking for Me because you are hungry and want Me to feed you again with more bread? Don't spend so much time looking for bread that won't satisfy your hunger. Spend more of your time looking for bread that will never make you hungry again."

"Where can we find this bread?" the people asked.

Jesus answered, "You must believe in Me, for I am the Bread of Life. If you believe that I am God's Son, you will never be hungry again."

But the people were not ready to believe in Jesus. "Show us some more miracles," they said. "Then we will believe in you. Give us bread every day like Moses did in the wilderness long ago."

"God gave that bread to you, not Moses," Jesus told the people. "But now God is offering you a new kind of bread. This bread comes straight from heaven, and it will change your life!"

"That's the kind of bread we want," the people shouted. "Where is it?"

"I already told you," Jesus said. "I am that bread. I cannot make it any easier for you to understand. If you believe that I am God's Son, then you will live with Me forever in heaven." Jesus was telling them that He could satisfy the hunger in their lives for God. And that is a stronger hunger than hunger for food.

When Jesus finished speaking, many of the people left Him. They did not want to believe that Jesus was God's Son. They only wanted to get something to eat and they thought Jesus would keep on giving them bread every day.

Several small boats from Tiberias were nearby, so when the people saw that Jesus wasn't there, nor His disciples, they got into the boats and went across to Capernaum to look for Him. John 6:23,24

Ruins of a synagogue at Capernaum have been uncovered and partially restored. This synagogue was built after the time of Christ on the same location as the synagogue which He visited. Peter's home has been uncovered a short distance from the synagogue. Jesus probably stayed in this home when He lived in Capernaum.

Jesus turned to talk to His disciples. "Are you going to leave Me, too?" He asked.

"Where else could we go?" Peter answered. "Only through You can we have eternal life. You have shown everyone that You are God's Son. We believe that You are."

Peter knew that Jesus was the only one who could truly share God's gift of eternal life with them. Later Peter would realize that he and his friends would be asked to share God's gift of eternal life with others.

You and I are also asked to share God's gift of eternal life by telling others about Jesus, the Bread of Life. So we should be like Jesus and tell others how they can have eternal life too.

Jesus replied, "The truth of the matter is that you want to be with Me because I fed you, not because you believe in Me. But you shouldn't be so concerned about perishable things like food. No, spend your energy seeking the eternal life, that I, the Messiah, can give you."
John 6:26,27

Think

1. Who is the Bread of Life? 2. What did Jesus mean when He said He is the Bread of Life? 3. What wonderful gift was Jesus sharing? 4. What wonderful gift can we share with others? 5. Will you?

Learn

From this story we learn that Jesus shared the wonderful gift of eternal life with others. We should do that, too.

Do

What can you use when you want to share God's gift to others? Unscramble this word and you will have the answer: ELIBB.

Answer: BIBLE

FORGIVING A SINFUL WOMAN
Like Jesus: FORGIVING OTHERS

Another great celebration was taking place in Jerusalem. It was the Feast of Tabernacles, and people came to the city from all over the land of Israel.

One of the most important places to go during the week-long celebration was the Temple. Jesus and His disciples went there every day. As usual, the crowds gathered around to hear Him teach.

Jesus taught them many important lessons. One of those lessons was about forgiving others. Soon He had a chance to show them what He meant.

Some men pushed their way into the Temple courtyard. With them was a woman who looked afraid. The men shoved her against one of the Temple walls. They picked up some large rocks on the ground. It looked as if they were going to kill her.

Then some of the men saw Jesus sitting nearby. They grabbed the woman and brought her to Him.

"Teacher, we caught this woman with someone else's husband," they said to Jesus. "According to the laws Moses wrote long ago, she should be stoned to death. What do you think we should do?"

Jesus looked at the men. He looked at the woman. Then He knelt down and began to draw in the dirt with His finger. Finally the men grew impatient and asked again. "Well, what should we do?" they demanded.

Jesus stood up. He looked at the men who were still holding the large rocks. "The one who has never sinned may throw the first rock," He said. Then Jesus knelt down and drew in the dirt again.

The men stood looking at Jesus. Of course they had sinned. No one in the world could say they were perfect. One by one they dropped their rocks and walked away.

Soon, the woman was left standing alone. Jesus walked over to her.

"Didn't anyone condemn you for what you did?" He asked her.

"No sir," she answered. "No one."

"Then I won't condemn you either," Jesus told her. "It is God, not man who should judge others. You have done a bad thing, but God will forgive you if you are sorry for what you have done. Go,

"Teacher," they said to Jesus, "this woman was caught in the very act of adultery. Moses' law says to kill her. What about it?" John 8:4-5

On the west side of modern
Jerusalem is a model of the city at
the time of Christ. The front of this
picture shows part of the large
Temple Court of the Gentiles. This
story probably took place here. In the
background is the Tower of Antonia
where Pilate judged Jesus. In the
center of the large courtyard were
other Temple courtyards and the
building with the Holy Place and
Holy of Holies.

and do not do it again."

As the woman left to go home, the people watched in
amazement. Jesus forgave her, even though she didn't deserve it.
Shouldn't we forgive others too?

71

Think

1. Why did the men want to hurt the woman? 2. Have any of your friends ever done something wrong to you? 3. What did Jesus do to the woman? 4. What should you do to your friends when they have done you wrong?

They were trying to trap Him into saying something they could use against Him, but Jesus stooped down and wrote in the dust with His finger. John 8:6

Then Jesus stood up again and said to her, "Where are your accusers? Didn't even one of them condemn you?"

"No sir," she said.

And Jesus said, "Neither do I. Go and sin no more." John 8:10-11

Learn

From this story we learn that Jesus forgave the woman even though she didn't deserve it, and that you should forgive others when they don't deserve it.

Do

Put a rock about the size of your hand on a shelf. Each time you look at it think about this story. It will remind you to forgive others.

JESUS HEALS A BLIND MAN

Like Jesus: HELPING OTHERS

n the street corner sat a blind man, begging for money and food.

"Why is this man blind?" the disciples asked Jesus. "Was this caused by his own sin or his parents' sins?"

"Just because you are sick or handicapped doesn't mean you have sinned," Jesus told them. "This man was born blind so that he might believe that I am God's Son."

Jesus knelt by the street corner and scooped up a handful of mud. He flattened the mud in His hands, and placed it on the blind man's eyes.

"Go wash your eyes in the Pool of Siloam over there," Jesus told the man.

With the help of his friends, the blind man walked over to the pool. He got on his knees and splashed the cool water over his eyes.

When the mud fell off his eyes he could see. "I can see! I can see!" the man shouted happily.

Crowds of people began to gather around the pool as the man jumped for joy. "Isn't that the blind beggar who sits on the street corner asking for food?" they asked. "No, it can't be the same man," said some. "Yes it is," said the others. "At least it looks like him."

Then the man shouted, "Yes! It's me! I'm not blind anymore."

"What happened?" the crowd asked.

"A man called Jesus put some mud on my eyes, and when I washed it off I could see," the man told them.

"Where is Jesus now?" they asked. But Jesus was nowhere to be found. He had slipped away into the crowd.

Then some evil men began to ask questions. They were angry at Jesus because He was getting so much attention.

"Jesus is a bad man," they said. "How can you say such good things about Him?"

"All I know is that I was blind, and Jesus helped me see," the man told them. "So how can you say He is evil?"

Later, Jesus went to find the man who had been blind. "Do you know who I am?" Jesus asked him.

"No, but I would like to," he replied.

"I healed you so that you would believe in Me, God's Son," Jesus said. "Do you believe?"

"...But while I am still here in the world, I give it My light." Then He spat on the ground and made mud from the spittle and smoothed the mud over the blind man's eyes.
John 9:5,6

In Jesus' time blindness was common, caused by insects that carried disease, unclean living conditions, poor sewage control, poor safety conditions that caused accidents, and hand-to-hand warfare that led to injuries. In this picture we see a blind man being led by an older boy. This was a common practice in Bible times, too. Jesus said once that blind people do not choose blind people to lead them.

"Yes, I believe," the man said to Jesus. Many others nearby believed in Jesus that day too. Jesus had helped a man when no one else could. Perhaps we, too, should help someone who really needs help.

Think

1. How did Jesus help the blind man? 2. Could anyone else do that? 3. Perhaps you are the only one who can help a friend. Will you help that person when he or she needs you?

[Jesus] told him, "Go and wash in the Pool of Siloam" (the word "Siloam" means "Sent"). So the man went where he was sent and washed and came back seeing!
John 9:7

Some of [the Pharisees] said, "Then this fellow Jesus is not from God, because He is working on the Sabbath." Others said, "But how could an ordinary sinner do such miracles?" John 9:16

Learn

From this story we learn that Jesus helped others when no one else could. We should do that, too.

Do

Did you know there are some things that no one but you can do? Nobody can love your parents the same way you do. Nobody can take your place with them either. What are some other things that only you can do?

JESUS THE GOOD SHEPHERD
Like Jesus: CARING FOR THOSE WE LOVE

What is Jesus like? What would you say to someone who never heard of Jesus before?

When Jesus came to earth He wanted to tell people who He was. But of course people could not understand it when He said He was God's Son. They could not understand it when He told them that He was God. How could that be?

While He was here on earth, Jesus compared Himself to many things that people understood. He told them that He was like water. People knew about water. It took away their thirst and kept them alive. He told them He was like bread. The people knew about bread, too. They knew they needed bread to stay alive.

One day Jesus told them that He was like a shepherd. "I am the Good Shepherd," Jesus said. People knew about shepherds. There were many at that time. They saw shepherds leading their sheep to food and water. They knew how much shepherds loved their sheep and how much sheep loved their shepherds. They knew how shepherds took care of the sheep that they loved so much.

"I will even give My life for My sheep," Jesus told them.

Some day Jesus would die on the cross for His people. That's what He meant when He said He would give His life for His sheep. How could anyone do more for those he loved?

Those of us who love Jesus follow Him, just as sheep follow their shepherd. We trust Jesus to lead us in the right places. And we know that some day He will lead us to His home in heaven. That's the kind of shepherd we should follow, isn't it?

"I am the Good Shepherd," Jesus said. He will take care of those whom He loves. We should be like Him, and take care of those we love, too, shouldn't we?

"I am the Good Shepherd and know My own sheep, and they know Me, just as My Father knows Me and I know the Father; and I lay down My life for the sheep..."
John 10:14-15

Think

1. Jesus compared Himself to many different things. Can you name some of them? 2. How does Jesus take care of those whom He loves? 3. How should we take care of those we love?

Learn

From this story we learn that Jesus the Good Shepherd takes care of those He loves.

Do

List each person in your family; also list your pets. Under each name, write one special thing you can do to help take care of that person or pet.

THE GOOD SAMARITAN

Like Jesus: LOVING OTHERS

One day, while Jesus was teaching, a teacher asked Him a question. "How can I live forever in heaven?" he said.

"What does God's Word say?" Jesus asked.

"That I must love God more than anything, and that I must love my neighbor as much as myself," he said.

The man thought for a moment. "Who are my neighbors?" he asked. Were they just the people next door?

Jesus answered by telling the man a story:

Once a Jewish man was taking a trip from Jerusalem to Jericho. Along the way a band of robbers attacked. They beat the man, took his money, and left him bleeding.

Before long a priest came down the road, saw the man, and walked to the other side. He would not stop to help.

A short time later, a helper in God's house came down the road. But he walked by the poor man too.

At last a Samaritan man came along. Samaritans and Jews did not like each other. They were always quarreling. But when the Samaritan saw the Jewish man hurt and bleeding, he had compassion and stopped to help.

The Samaritan washed the man's cuts and put bandages on them. Then he put the man on his donkey and took him to a nearby inn.

"Take care of this man," the Samaritan told the innkeeper. "I will pay whatever it costs."

When Jesus finished, the teacher knew who his neighbors were. *Everyone* was his neighbor, whether he loved the person or not. Jesus loved all His neighbors, even those who did not love Him! Should we?

The Samaritan…put the man on his donkey and walked along beside him till they came to an inn, where he nursed him through the night.
Luke 10:34

Think

1. Who walked by without helping the man who was hurt?
2. Who stopped to help? 3. Which was a good neighbor? Why?
4. How does Jesus want us to be good neighbors?

Luke 10:25-37

Learn

From this story we learn that Jesus loved others, even those who did not love Him.

Do

Can you think of one person who does not love you? What can you do to show love to that person? Will you?

JESUS TELLS HOW TO PRAY
Like Jesus: PRAYING THE RIGHT WAY

Whenever He could, Jesus found a quiet place to be alone with God and talk with Him.

One day the disciples asked Jesus to teach them how to pray, too. So Jesus sat down with them and taught them a simple prayer. We have come to know this as The Lord's Prayer. Actually, some people call it The Disciples' Prayer because it was a prayer to help the disciples. Here is that simple prayer that Jesus taught.

"When you pray," Jesus said, "say something like this:

"Our Father in heaven, how wonderful is Your holy name. We look forward to the day when we will live with You forever in heaven. Give us enough food for each day. And forgive us when we sin, just as we forgive anyone who hurts. Help us not to be tempted to do things we know are wrong."

Then Jesus told the disciples a story to help them understand prayer better:

Suppose you went to a friend's house in the middle of the night and asked him for some extra food for a surprise guest. What would you think if your friend called back, "Go home! I won't come down to help you"?

Then suppose you kept on knocking, and your friend came to the door and gave you what you wanted.

"This is the way you should pray," Jesus told His disciples. "If there is something you really need, keep asking God and He will answer your prayer. For God is ready to give you many wonderful things if you will only ask Him."

Jesus knew how to pray the right way, didn't He? That's why we should learn from Him.

Once when Jesus had been out praying, one of His disciples came to Him as He finished and said, "Lord, teach us a prayer to recite just as John taught one to his disciples." Luke 11:1

Think

1. Why does Jesus know how to pray? Did He pray very much?
2. Why should we learn how to pray from Jesus?

Luke 11:1-13

Learn

From this story we learn that Jesus knew the right way to pray, and if we want to know the right way, we will learn from Him.

Do

Memorize The Lord's Prayer (Matthew 6:9-13) from your favorite translation.

HEALING ON THE SABBATH

Like Jesus: SHOWING KINDNESS

I f you had gone to God's house with Jesus, you would have found things much different from today. In those days God's house was called a synagogue and everyone went there on Saturday, which was called the Sabbath.

The Sabbath was a special day. He knew how hard the people worked during the week. He knew how busy they were doing the ordinary things that must be done. By the end of each week everyone was tired and needed a rest.

So God made the Sabbath for rest and worship. He wanted people to rest from their hard work. He wanted them to worship Him on a peaceful day.

But the Pharisees, who were the religious leaders, decided they should tell the people how to rest and worship. So they made a long list of rules. They made so many rules that they couldn't even remember them all.

Jesus did not like all these rules. He knew that God made the Sabbath a day of rest and worship, not a day of rules.

One day someone asked Jesus to teach in one of the synagogues. As He was talking to the people He noticed an old woman who was bent over as if she was in pain.

Jesus found that she was cripped. For the last eighteen years she had not been able to stand up straight.

Jesus felt compassion for the woman and called her to the front of the synagogue. "Dear woman," He said to her, "I am going to heal you." Then Jesus touched her and at once she stood up straight.

The crowd was amazed at what Jesus had done. But the synagogue leaders were jealous because they couldn't do what

One Sabbath as He was teaching in the synagogue, He saw a seriously handicapped woman who had been bent double for eighteen years and was unable to straighten herself. Luke 13:10

Think

1. How was Jesus kind to the crippled woman? 2. How could He have been hurt by being kind to her? 3. Why do you think He was kind anyway? 4. Why should you be kind even when it could hurt you?

Jesus had done.

One of them stood up and spoke to the crowd. "If anyone else wants to be healed," he shouted, "come back some other day. This Jesus is breaking our laws by healing people on the Sabbath. He is working, not resting." Jesus said to the Jewish leaders, "You do not even obey your own rules. That means you are hypocrites! You work on the Sabbath when you take your cattle from their stalls and lead them out for water. Yet you say it is wrong for Me to free this woman from the bondage Satan has held her in for eighteen years!"

Jesus' words shamed the Jewish leaders. But the crowds were happy and shared the woman's joy. The people had again seen Jesus perform a miracle. And again they had heard Jesus say that helping others should be more important than any religious rules.

Jesus was angry with these grumpy men as He should be. Whenever He showed kindness toward someone, these men caused trouble. They didn't want Jesus to be kind to people because it made Jesus look good. They didn't like that. They wanted to look good instead.

These men could have caused a lot of trouble for Jesus. They could have hurt Him. But Jesus was kind to the woman anyway. That was the right thing to do.

Learn

From this story we learn that Jesus was kind even when He could have been hurt.

Do

Read this story again, but pretend you are there instead of Jesus and that the Pharisees are some "friends" who would hurt you. What would you do then?

THE BOY WHO RAN AWAY
Like Jesus: FORGIVING OTHERS

One day Jesus told a story about a boy who ran away. Jesus said: Once there was a boy who got tired of living at home. He had a good father and a good brother. He lived in a beautiful home. But the boy grew tired of being good. He wanted to do whatever pleased him.

So the boy told his father he was leaving home. "Please give me all the money I will inherit from you some day," he asked.

The father did not want to give his boy the money. But he knew his son needed to learn an important lesson.

So the boy took lots of money from his father and went on a long trip. He did whatever made him feel good. He spent money on many new friends.

One day, when the boy reached for his money, it was gone. He had spent it all. Now what would he do?

Soon he became hungry. Then he became lonely. His new "friends" did not want to be his friends now that he had no money.

Suddenly the boy did not feel good any more. He knew now that doing what he wanted didn't make him happy. He wanted to go home but he knew how foolish he had been.

The boy soon realized that there was no other place to go. So he headed home. While he was still far from home, his father saw him coming and ran and hugged him and kissed him.

"Father, I'm sorry," the boy said. "I'm not good enough to be your son. Let me be one of your servants."

"But you ARE my son," the father said. "I will forgive you."

The boy was happy that his father forgave him. Jesus told the story to show that this is what we should do.

While he was still a long distance away, his father saw him coming, and was filled with loving pity and ran and embraced him and kissed him. Luke 15:20

Think

1. What did the boy do that was wrong? 2. Why did the father forgive him? 3. Why should we forgive others, even when they have done wrong?

Luke 15:11-32

Learn

From this story we learn that Jesus wants us to forgive, no matter what others have done to us.

Do

Write the names of one or two people who have done something wrong to you. Next to each name, write the day this week you will pray for them. When they ask, forgive them. If they don't, ask God to help you forgive them anyway, and keep praying for them.

THE RICH MAN AND LAZARUS
Like Jesus: KNOWING THE WAY TO HEAVEN

o you remember the last time you were hot and thirsty? Do you remember how much you wanted something cool to drink? One day Jesus told a story about a rich man who longed for a drink of cool water, but who never got one.

There was once a rich man who had everything he wanted. He had so much money he didn't know what to do with it.

In the same town lived a poor beggar named Lazarus. One day Lazarus' friends laid him on the doorstep of the rich man's house, hoping the man would be kind to poor Lazarus and give him some food.

But Lazarus never received anything more than scraps from the rich man's table. And his only medicine was from the dogs that licked his sores.

Finally, Lazarus died, and was lovingly carried to heaven by angels. He would spend eternity with Abraham, in the place where all who believed and lived good lives went before Jesus died and made a place for believers.

The rich man died, too. But his soul went to hell, to spend eternity in pain and suffering.

The rich man was surprised to be in hell. On earth, he was rich and important, and Lazarus was poor and diseased and ordinary.

When the rich man looked up, he saw Lazarus in heaven, far away. Next to him sat Abraham. Why was Lazarus in heaven and not him?

The rich man called to Abraham. "Abraham, have pity on me," he cried. "I am hot and thirsty. If Lazarus could only dip his finger in a cup of cool water and place it on my tongue, I would be happy."

One day Lazarus, a diseased beggar, was laid at his door. As he lay there longing for scraps from the rich man's table, the dogs would come and lick his open sores.
Luke 16:20,21

Think

1. Who knows the way to heaven? 2. Why should we listen when Jesus talks about heaven? 3. Why is it important to help others know Jesus?

Abraham called back to the rich man, "In your lifetime you had everything you wanted, and Lazarus had nothing. Yet, you refused to share with him. Now you must stay there and Lazarus will stay here.

"I have five brothers," the rich man called back across the deep pit separating heaven and hell. "Send someone to warn them about this."

"Even if someone dies to pay for their sins, and then rises from the dead and shows them the way to heaven," Abraham said, "your brothers will not believe in Him because they don't want to give up their sinful ways."

Jesus told this story to the Pharisees, those rich and important men who didn't care about ordinary people. He knew that even when He died for their sins, and then rose from the dead, the Pharisees would not believe in Him.

Jesus is the only one who knows the way to heaven. That's because He *is* the way. When we know Him, as our Savior, we know the only way to heaven.

Learn

From this story we learn that Jesus knows the way to heaven and He wants us to know Him so we can be with Him there, and so we will know the way there.

Do

Memorize Jesus' words in John 14:6. Quote it the next time someone wants to know the way to heaven.

JESUS RAISES LAZARUS

Like Jesus: SHOWING COMPASSION

What should we do?" Mary and Martha wondered as they watched their brother Lazarus. He was sick, and with each passing day he was getting worse.

The two sisters looked helplessly at each other. Then they looked at their brother. They were sure that he was dying.

"We must send for Jesus at once," Martha suggested. "He is the only one who can help Lazarus now."

Before long a friend hurried away to find Jesus, who was visiting in a place far away. When the man found Jesus, he told Him Lazarus was very sick. Of course he did not know that Lazarus had already died while he was looking for Jesus.

"Please hurry," said the man. "We all love Lazarus and want him to live."

Jesus loved Lazarus, too. But He did not go with the man that day. He wanted people to know that God could bring someone back to life after several days.

Later, Jesus and His disciples headed toward Lazarus' home. "Lazarus is dead now," Jesus told them. "But there is a good reason why this has happened. Come and you will find out what it is."

When Martha heard that Jesus was near her town, she ran out to meet Him. "If only you had come in time," she said. "My brother would not have died."

"But Lazarus will live again," Jesus told her.

"I know he will live again when God raises all His people to life," said Martha.

"I am the One who raises people from the dead," said Jesus. "People who believe in Me never truly die. Do you believe this?"

"Of course," said Martha. "I know you are God's Son." But Martha didn't really understand what Jesus was saying.

Martha went home and told her sister Mary that Jesus had come. Mary hurried out to meet Him and fell down at His feet. Mary was crying.

"If only you had come earlier," she said. "Lazarus would not have died."

Jesus looked with compassion at Mary. He knew how deeply she hurt inside. Then Jesus looked at Lazarus' friends who had come with Mary. They were sad and hurt too, and they were crying.

When Martha got word that Jesus was coming, she went to meet Him. But Mary stayed at home. Martha said to Jesus, "Sir, if you had been here, my brother wouldn't have died..." John 11:20,21

The tomb pictured here, near
Bethany where Lazarus lived, is like
many burial caves in Jesus' time.
Caves provided a natural tomb where
several people in a family could be
buried. Sometimes a large rolling
stone was placed over the cave
entrance to keep out robbers.

Tears came to Jesus' eyes. Some of the men standing nearby saw Him crying. "They must have been good friends," the men said. "See how much Jesus loved him. But couldn't He have kept Lazarus from dying?"

Mary and Martha slowly led Jesus to the tomb where Lazarus was buried. It was a cave with a large stone rolled in front of the opening.

"Roll that stone away," said Jesus.

"Do you really want to do that?" Martha asked. "Lazarus has been dead more than four days."

Martha was concerned because people in that hot land were buried the same day they died. They did not treat their bodies, so they began to decay quickly.

"Didn't I tell you that you would see wonderful things?" said Jesus.

So the men rolled the stone away. Then Jesus prayed and shouted.

"Lazarus! Come out!" He called.

People stared at the empty hole that led into the dark cave where Lazarus was buried. Suddenly Lazarus appeared at the doorway, still dressed from head to foot in his graveclothes.

"Unwrap him, so he can be with his sisters," Jesus commanded. The crowd was amazed at what they had seen Jesus do.

"Surely this must be God's Son," many said.

Even some troublemakers believed! What a wonderful day of joy, not only for Mary, Martha, and Lazarus, but for those who came to believe in Jesus.

That day many people saw Jesus show compassion to Lazarus and his friends when they hurt. We need to remember that when those around us hurt, we, too, should show compassion to them.

So they rolled the stone aside. Then Jesus looked up to heaven and said, "Father, thank You for hearing Me. (You always hear Me, of course, but I said it because of all these people standing here, so that they will believe You sent Me.)" Then He shouted, "Lazarus, come out!" John 11:41-42

Think

1. Why were Mary and Martha so sad? 2. How do you know that Jesus felt compassion for them? 3. How did Jesus show compassion for these people? 4. What can you do when your friends are hurting?

Learn

From this story we learn that Jesus showed compassion to others when they hurt. We should do that, too.

Do

Think of a friend who is hurting or sad. Pick up the phone now and call that person. Say, "I'm your friend. I'm praying for you." Or write the same message on a card and mail it to your friend. Then be sure to pray for that person.

JESUS HEALS TEN LEPERS
Like Jesus: GIVING A SECOND GIFT

I t's not fun to be sick, and it was especially bad for those who lived in Jesus' time. Back then they had no hospitals or medicines to help them. Many people who got sick never got well. Doctors could not help them.

People who got sick with leprosy were sent out of town so other people wouldn't catch leprosy too. This is what happened to ten men whom Jesus met one day.

When they became sick, they were sent out of town. There was no one to help them.

One day it happened. Jesus was coming to their town! They had heard that Jesus made sick people well again! But the lepers lived outside town. How could they get to see Jesus! The people would not let them near the town.

But the ten lepers knew they had to try. They crept as close to town as they dared.

"Jesus! Jesus!" they shouted from a distance. "Please help us, for no one else can."

"You are healed," Jesus told them. "Now show a priest that you are well so the people will let you live in town again."

As the men ran into town, they noticed that they were completely well. One of the men stopped as the others raced ahead. He hurried back and fell on his knees before Jesus.

"Praise God, I'm healed!" he said to Jesus. "Thank you!"

But something else happened to the man who came back. He believed in Jesus as God's Son. The other nine men were satisfied to be healed. But this man received a second special gift from Jesus. Jesus gave him a new life when the man believed in Him. That's like Jesus, isn't it? Wouldn't you like to be like that too?

One of them came back to Jesus, shouting, "Glory to God, I'm healed!" He fell flat on the ground in front of Jesus, face downward in the dust, thanking Him for what He had done.
Luke 17:15,16

Think

1. Why were the lepers living outside town? 2. What did Jesus do for them? 3. What did the one man do to say thank you? 4. What second gift did he receive from Jesus? Do you do nice things when someone says thank you?

Learn

From this story we learn that we may want to give a second special gift when people say thank you. Jesus did.

Do

What are some special second gifts you can give when people say thank you? Here are some ideas: a smile, a hug, saying "you are welcome," your friendship. Can you name some others?

TWO MEN WENT TO PRAY

Like Jesus: HELPING PEOPLE KNOW

 Most people want to be right. Nobody wants to be wrong. Think about your friends. Do you have friends who want to be right? Do you have any friends who really want to be wrong?

It's good to want to be right. But it's not so good to think we are always right.

Jesus knew some people like that. They thought they were right all the time. That made them feel that they were important. They were called Pharisees, the religious leaders of the people in Jesus' land.

The Pharisees thought they were right about how people should act toward God. They knew more about the laws of Moses than most people. So most people thought they were right when they said something. This made the Pharisees do strange things, such as pretend to be more important than anyone else. They also decided it was their job to make up lots of rules. Before long they thought their rules were as important as God's laws.

The Pharisees also did something else strange. When they listened to Jesus teach about God, they became angry. When they saw Him heal people or raise them from the dead, they became jealous. Wouldn't you think these men would fall on their knees and worship Jesus? But they didn't.

When people heard Jesus teach, they listened carefully. Nobody else had lived in heaven. Nobody else had lived with God. That's why the things Jesus said seemed right when people heard them.

But the more people listened to Jesus, the more angry and jealous the Pharisees became. One day Jesus told a story so the Pharisees would hear it:

Two men went into the Temple to pray. One was a Pharisee.

"I tell you, this sinner, not the Pharisee, returned home forgiven! For the proud shall be humbled, but the humble shall be honored."
Luke 18:14

Think

1. Why didn't the Pharisees like Jesus? 2. What did Jesus try to tell the Pharisees and others? 3. Who listened? Who did not? 4. How can we help others know how to be right?

He thought he was right. He walked into the Temple where everyone would see him. Then he prayed loud so everyone would hear him.

"Thank you God that I am not a sinner like everyone else here," he prayed.

The other man was a tax collector. Nobody liked tax collectors. So he went into a corner where no one else would see him. He knew he was a sinner.

"Dear God," he prayed. "I know I have sinned and I am sorry. Please forgive me and have mercy on me."

When the two men went home the tax collector was truly happy, for he knew his sins were forgiven. But the Pharisee was probably not happy, for he thought that he had no sins, and that was the biggest sin of all. If he thought he had no sins, how could he think they were forgiven?

When Jesus finished His story he looked at the Pharisees, standing there in the crowd. "You are wrong to think you are always right," Jesus told them. Jesus wanted the Pharisees to realize how wrong they were so they could ask God to help them be right.

The Pharisees wouldn't listen to Jesus. But some ordinary people did. They knew they were sinners. They asked Jesus to forgive their sins. Even though they had been wrong because of their sins, they were more right now than the Pharisees.

Jesus tried to help people know when they were wrong. The Pharisees were foolish because they wouldn't listen. Some ordinary people were wise, because they did listen.

Learn

From this story we learn that Jesus helped others know when they were right or wrong.

Do

Find some red and green construction paper. Give one piece of each color to each person in your family. Play a family game by naming things that people often do. Each person flashes green (right) or red (wrong) to show what they think about each thing.

JESUS AND THE CHILDREN

Like Jesus: WILLING TO SERVE

 lmost everyone wanted to be near Jesus. He was always doing things for others. He made sick people well. He made blind people see. He made friends with lonely people. He gave food to hungry people. And He told wonderful stories about God. He told people how they could live forever with God in heaven. No wonder people wanted to be near Jesus!

Little children wanted to be with Jesus too. They loved His kind smile and gentle words. One day some mothers brought their children to see Jesus. But when the disciples saw the mothers coming, they stopped them.

"Don't bother Jesus," they told the mothers. "He is too busy to spend time talking with children."

The disciples thought that Jesus was too important to be bothered by children. There were many grown-ups who needed Jesus' help, and many important leaders who wanted to talk with Him.

Jesus heard what the disciples said to the mothers and children. "No!" Jesus said. "Don't send the children away. Bring them to Me."

Jesus loved children. He laughed with them, and played with them. They could talk with Him any time they wanted to. Jesus put the babies and the little children on His lap. He put His arms around the bigger children and taught them when they wanted to learn. He even told them stories to make them happy and help them understand God's love for them.

Then, He placed His hands on the children's shoulders and prayed for them. His desire was for each one to grow to be wise, and to love God as He did.

"Let the children come to me, for the Kingdom of God belongs to such as they. Don't send them away! I tell you as seriously as I know how that anyone who refuses to come to God as a little child will never be allowed into His Kingdom. Mark 10:14,15

Think

1. What did Jesus think of children? 2. What did He say about them? 3. Why did Jesus ask the rich young man to sell what he had and follow him?

Jesus loved the children. And He loves you, too. But the disciples did not understand why He loved them so.

"If you want to be really important," Jesus told the disciples, "you must be like these children. They come to me with an open mind, and believe all that I tell them. And besides that, they are always ready to do what I ask."

After a while the children left to go home. As Jesus was walking down the road he met a rich man. "Jesus," the man asked, "what must I do to have eternal life and live forever with You in heaven?"

"You know what God's Word says," Jesus told him. "You are to keep His commandments. That means don't lie, don't steal, honor your mother and father, and love your neighbor as yourself."

"But I have done all these things," the man told Jesus.

Then Jesus looked into the man's eyes. "There is one more thing you need to do," He said to him. "Sell all your things, and follow Me."

The man looked down at the ground. He didn't want to do what Jesus asked, for he had many, many wonderful things.

Perhaps Jesus wasn't really asking the man to give up everything he had. He was trying to help the man see what was most important in his life. Jesus knew that sometimes we may have to give up some of our favorite things in order to help or serve others. The rich man was not ready to do that. Are you?

Learn

From this story we learn that we should be willing to serve others.

Do

Ask mother or father to help you cut a picture of a child and another picture of a rich man from a magazine. Mount these on construction paper and hang them on the wall for a few days to remind you of these two stories.

JESUS HEALS A BLIND MAN
Like Jesus: WANTING TO HELP OTHERS

Jesus and His disciples were on their way to Jerusalem. As Jesus walked ahead, the disciples followed, nervous and afraid. "Why does Jesus want to go to Jerusalem?" they asked each other. "The Pharisees and their friends want to hurt Him."

Jesus heard what they were saying. He knew the answer to their question. The work that God had given Him to do on earth would soon be over. But Jesus had to go to Jerusalem to finish it.

Jesus tried to tell His disciples what would happen when they reached Jerusalem.

"When we get to the city, I will be arrested by the religious leaders and sentenced to die," Jesus said. "They will make fun of Me, spit on Me, and drag Me out of the city to kill Me. But after three days I will rise again from the dead."

Somehow the disciples could not understand what Jesus was trying to say. They did not understand that this would all happen to Him, and that this was part of God's wonderful plan to save people from their sins.

Along the way Jesus and the disciples came to the town of Jericho. By this time a large crowd was following Him.

Near the city gate sat a blind man named Bartimaeus. Each day he sat there, begging those who passed by for food or money.

Bartimaeus heard the crowd coming down the road. "What is going on?" he asked.

"Jesus is coming," someone answered.

Bartimaeus had heard about Jesus. He had heard people tell stories about the wonderful things Jesus had done. Bartimaeus knew that Jesus cared for others and wanted to help them.

"O Teacher," the blind man said, "I want to see!"

And Jesus said to him, "All right, it's done. Your faith has healed you." And instantly the blind man could see, and followed Jesus down the road! Mark 11:51,52

Think

1. What was wrong with Bartimaeus? 2. What did Jesus do to help him? 3. Why do you think Jesus cared about others and wanted to help them?

Perhaps Jesus would help him.

As the crowd passed by, Bartimaeus began shouting as loud as he could, "Jesus! Jesus! Have mercy on me."

Some people nearby scolded Bartimaeus. "Be quiet!" they told him. They didn't want a blind beggar to keep Jesus from more important things.

But Bartimaeus shouted even louder. He might never again have a chance to see.

Jesus heard Bartimaeus. He stopped and listened. "Bring Me that man who is calling My name," He said.

Somebody took Bartimaeus' hand and brought him to Jesus. Everybody could see that Jesus cared about blind Bartimaeus and wanted to help him.

"You called for Me," Jesus said to him. "What would you like Me to do?"

"Jesus, I want to see," Bartimaeus said.

"Because you believed that I could help you, your eyes are now healed," Jesus told him.

At once Bartimaeus could see. He was no longer a blind beggar. "I want to follow You," he told Jesus. And he did.

Learn

From this story we learn that Jesus cared about others and wanted to help them.

Do

Close your eyes for a full minute. Pretend you are blind Bartimaeus. What would you like Jesus to do for you? Perhaps you are blind and may not be healed. What else would you like Jesus to do for you?

ZACCHAEUS CLIMBS A TREE
Like Jesus: BEING FRIENDLY

Zacchaeus was a tax collector who lived in Jericho. Each day he sat in his booth by the side of the road so the people could come pay their taxes. But Zacchaeus was not honest. He made the people pay more than they should, and he became rich. The people did not like him.

On a certain day Zacchaeus heard that Jesus had come to Jericho.

"Who is this Jesus?" Zacchaeus asked. "I want to see him."

Suddenly Zacchaeus heard something. He leaned over his tax booth and looked down the road. A crowd of people was coming.

"Jesus is coming! Jesus is coming!" people shouted.

At last Zacchaeus was going to see Jesus. But as the crowd came near, Zacchaeus couldn't see Jesus at all. Jesus was in the middle of the crowd, and Zacchaeus was too short to see over all those people.

Quickly Zacchaeus ran to a sycamore tree beside the road. He climbed up into the tree and waited for the crowd to pass by. As the people came near, Zacchaeus saw Jesus. Jesus saw Zacchaeus too.

"Zacchaeus, climb down from that tree," Jesus said to him. "I want to go to your house today."

Then Zacchaeus believed in Jesus. He was glad Jesus wanted to be his friend. And he was so sorry for all the wrong things he had done that he paid back everyone he had cheated.

The people were amazed when they saw the new Zacchaeus. Now they knew why Jesus wanted to be his friend. Do you know someone like Zacchaeus who might change if he knew Jesus?

When Jesus came by He looked up at Zacchaeus and called him by name! "Zacchaeus!" He said. "Quick! Come down! For I am going to be a guest in your home today!" Luke 19:5

Think

1. What kind of man was Zacchaeus at first? 2. How did he change? 3. Why was Jesus friendly to him? 4. What happened to Zacchaeus when Jesus came to his house?

Learn

From this story we learn that our being friendly to someone who isn't popular may help that person want to know more about Jesus, and Jesus can change that person's life completely.

Do

Read this story again. Instead of Zacchaeus' name say the name of someone who needs your friendship. Think of yourself as a friend of Jesus there beside him. How do you think the story will end?

RIDING INTO JERUSALEM
Like Jesus: DOING WHAT GOD WANTS

E ver since Jesus raised Lazarus from the dead, people had been talking about it. Not one of them had ever seen a person brought back to life. But Jesus had done it. Now, wherever people got together, they talked about this wonderful thing that had happened.

Most people were excited about what Jesus had done. They knew an ordinary man could not do this. Jesus had some special power and they wanted to know more about it. And they wanted to know more about Him. So people followed Jesus wherever He went. They listened to Him teach.

But not everyone felt this way about Jesus. Some grumpy men did not like Him. They listened to Him teach. But what He said made them angry and jealous.

Jesus could have been afraid of these grumpy men. They were important people. They dressed in special clothes that showed how important they were. They could make a lot of trouble for Jesus. They could even stir up enough trouble to have Him killed.

But Jesus was not afraid of them. He would do what God wanted Him to do, no matter what these men said or did.

Jesus' friends worried about Him, though. Some had warned Him not to come to the big celebration called the Passover. People came to Jerusalem every year for this, with friends and family. They ate and talked. There would be thousands of people swarming the streets of the city. It was like a big family reunion. But it would be a dangerous time for Jesus, for those important men could stir people against Him to kill Him.

But Jesus decided to come to the Passover anyway. Six days before it started, He came to Bethany, where He had raised Lazarus from the dead. There some friends had a big dinner for Him. News traveled to Jerusalem and crowds soon gathered to see this man who had raised a friend from the dead.

One day Jesus sent two of His disciples to a friend's house for a donkey. "You will see the donkey just as you enter town," Jesus told them. "It will have a young colt with it. Untie them both and bring them here. If anyone asks what you are doing, tell them I needed them. It will be all right."

The disciples went and found the donkey and colt, just as Jesus had said. Jesus would ride on this colt as the Scriptures had said many years before, "The king will come riding into Jerusalem on a donkey's colt."

A huge crowd of Passover visitors took palm branches and went down the road to meet Him, shouting, "The Savior! God bless the King of Israel! Hail to God's Ambassador!" John 12:12,13

In Bible times the donkey, or ass, was
a common form of transportation.
When a family had to travel, the
donkey carried the goods and the
woman or child. The man walked. In
peacetime a king often rode an ass
because the horse was viewed as an
animal of war. Zechariah 9:9
prophesied that Christ would come
riding on a donkey Christ actually
rode on a young animal, the colt of
a donkey.

The disciples put some of their clothing on the colt so that Jesus could ride on it. Then Jesus began to ride toward Jerusalem.

People crowded around the colt from every direction. Many threw their robes on the path ahead of Jesus. Others cut branches from the trees and put them on the path too.

People began shouting, "God bless King David's Son, the Man of God is here. Praise God in heaven." It was a welcome fit for a king! These people made so much noise that it stirred the whole city of Jerusalem.

"Who is this?" some asked.

"Jesus of Nazareth!" was the answer.

Even the little children in the Temple began shouting, "God bless the Son of David!"

Of course this made the grumpy leaders angry and even more jealous. "Don't you hear what these children are saying?" they demanded.

"Yes," said Jesus. "I hear them. But haven't you ever read God's Word? It says even the smallest children will praise Me."

This made these men even more angry and they wanted to see Jesus killed. They were sure that they could find a way to do it. But Jesus would not let their evil plans keep Him from doing what God wanted Him to do.

Each day he went into God's house and taught the people about God. He was willing to do this no matter what happened.

And those in the crowd who had seen Jesus call Lazarus back to life were telling all about it. That was the main reason why so many went out to meet Him—because they had heard about this mighty miracle. John 12:17,18

Think

1. Who wanted to hurt Jesus? 2. Did Jesus hide from them or stay away from them? Why not? 3. Are you willing to do what God wants you to do, even if someone makes fun of you?

John 11:55–12:1

Learn

From this story we learn that Jesus did what God wanted Him to do, no matter what would happen.

Do

Should you tell a friend about Jesus? Perhaps you haven't because you are afraid. Write down the three worst things that could happen if you did. Should these keep you from doing this?

107

TEACHING IN THE TEMPLE
Like Jesus: ACCEPTING NEW FRIENDS

I t was Passover time again. Most of the people who came to Jerusalem were Jews. But some Greeks and Romans also came, for they wanted to worship God, too.

Some of the Greek people went to the Temple, God's house. Each day they listened to Jesus tell about God and His home in heaven. They began to realize that Jesus could help them know God.

These Greeks wanted to know God and know how to get to His home. They wanted to follow Jesus and be His disciples.

But would Jesus talk with them if they went to see Him? Would He care about them, or would he only talk to the Jewish people?

The Greeks went first to see Philip, one of Jesus' disciples. Perhaps he would help them.

"May we talk to Jesus?" they asked.

Philip didn't know what to say. Would Jesus accept the Greeks as His new friends? Most of the Jewish people at that time thought the Greeks were ungodly. Most did not think God would accept them.

Philip found Andrew and told him what the Greeks wanted. Then Philip and Andrew talked to Jesus.

"Whoever wants to be My friend and follow Me is welcome," Jesus told them.

Jesus did not care if the men were Greeks or Romans or Jews or something else. If they wanted to accept Him, He would accept them.

The Greeks were so happy that Jesus would be their friend. After the Passover they wanted to go home and tell their friends about Him.

"If these Greeks want to be My disciples, tell them to come and follow Me, for My servants must be where I am. And if they follow Me, the Father will honor them...."
John 12:26

Think

1. Who wanted to be Jesus' new friends? 2. Why were they afraid He might not accept them as His friends? 3. What did Jesus do? 4. What should we do when someone wants to be our new friend?

Learn

From this story we learn that Jesus accepted new friends.

Do

Tomorrow will you try to find a new friend? How will you do this? Talk with Mother or Father about this.

A WOMAN GIVES EVERYTHING
Like Jesus: GIVING BECAUSE OF LOVE

Jesus was at the Temple. He spent lots of time there because it was God's house. He felt especially close to God there.

One day Jesus stood near the Temple entrance. He watched the people come in and out. He watched them carefully. Some came to worship God. Here, they felt close to God, just as Jesus did.

Others came to the Temple to look important. They wore beautiful clothes. When they prayed, they made sure everyone was watching. They didn't want to be close to God. But they wanted everyone else to think they were close to Him.

In one part of the Temple there was a room where people gave their money. Along the walls were money boxes shaped like horns. People put their money in these boxes. The money was a gift to God.

As Jesus watched, he saw a rich man put lots of money into a money box. The disciples watched too. They were amazed at how much money the man put into the box.

"What a wonderful man," they must have thought. "Look how much he has given to God."

Then another rich man came along. He put more money into a money box than the first man. "God must be very pleased with these men," the disciples thought again.

The disciples watched to see who would be next to put money into a box. Jesus was watching too.

Through the Temple doors came a woman. She did not have beautiful clothes. Jesus knew that she was a poor widow. He watched as the widow walked up to the money box and dropped two small coins into it.

He called His disciples to Him and remarked, "That poor widow has given more than all those rich men put together! For they gave a little of their extra fat, while she gave up her last penny." Mark 12:43-44

Think

1. Why did Jesus say the poor woman gave more than the rich men? 2. What did Jesus think of her gift? 3. What are some things you can give to Jesus?

Jesus called to His disciples. "Were you watching when the woman put her money into a money box? She put more into the box than those two rich men before her."

The disciples were surprised! "How can that be?" they must have thought. They saw how much the rich men had put in the money box.

Then Jesus told them what He meant. "The rich men put lots of money into the box. But they had much more left over. The poor widow only had two small coins. She gave everything to God."

Jesus told the disciples that the rich men gave so they could get praise from the people watching. But the poor widow gave because she loved God.

It would seem that God would be more pleased with big gifts. But that is not what Jesus said. He said that God does not care how big or small a gift is. But He wants us to give because we love Him and want to give to Him. Do you?

Learn

From this story we learn that Jesus was glad for those who gave because they loved God.

Do

What are some important gifts you can give to Jesus? Draw five circles to represent five coins. In each write something you can give to Jesus.

MARY ANOINTS JESUS' FEET

Like Jesus: ACCEPTING GIFTS

A man named Simon gave a big dinner to honor Jesus. Simon lived in Bethany, near Jerusalem. Mary, Martha, and Lazarus also lived in Bethany. They came to the dinner too.

It seemed as if all of Jesus' friends were at the dinner. Martha served the food as everyone sat at the table, laughing and telling stories.

After dinner, Mary stood up and walked over to Jesus. She held a beautiful jar in her hands. The jar was filled with some wonderful perfume.

Mary loved Jesus very much. She wanted to show Jesus how much she loved Him. The jar of perfume was the very best thing she owned. She wanted to give her best to Jesus.

Mary opened the jar and poured the perfume over Jesus' head. Then she poured some on His feet and wiped them with her hair.

Some of the other men at the table became angry at Mary. "Why did she waste such expensive perfume?" they asked. "We could have sold it and given the money to the poor." The men did not like the way Mary used the perfume. They were not happy about what she did.

But Jesus said, "Don't be angry with Mary. She gave Me a wonderful gift."

Jesus also told the disciples that Mary was preparing His body for burial. Mary's gift was special to Jesus. He even told the disciples that she would be remembered forever for this gift.

Jesus was thankful for Mary's good gift. He wanted the other men to be thankful when they received good gifts too. Aren't you thankful when someone gives you a good gift?

Jesus knew what they were thinking, and said, "Why are you criticizing her? For she has done a good thing to Me. You will always have the poor among you, but you won't always have Me. Matthew 26:10,11

Think

1. What wonderful gift did Mary give to Jesus? 2. How did Jesus accept it? 3. How should you accept gifts that others give to you?

Learn

From this story we learn that Jesus accepted gifts with thanks. We should do that, too.

Do

Draw six little boxes that look like gifts wrapped in paper. On each write one of these letters: T H A N K S. What will these help you remember?

PREPARING THE LAST SUPPER
Like Jesus: ASKING FRIENDS TO HELP US

Excitement filled the air as the city of Jerusalem prepared to celebrate the Passover Feast.

Jesus and His disciples were staying nearby in Bethany. Soon they would go into Jerusalem to eat the Passover meal.

"Where will we eat our Passover meal?" the disciples asked.

Jesus looked at Peter and John. They liked doing things for Jesus. They helped Him whenever they could.

"Go to Jerusalem," Jesus told Peter and John. "When you get there, you will meet a man carrying a jug of water. Follow him home and say to the owner, 'Our Master needs a place to eat the Passover meal. Do you have a room?' He will then show you a room on the upper floor of his house. It will be ready for us."

Peter and John did just what Jesus said. They were glad to help.

When Peter and John came to Jerusalem, they saw a man carrying a jug of water. "That must be the man Jesus told us to find," they said. So they followed the man home.

There Peter and John asked the owner if he had a room in which they could eat the Passover meal. They said what Jesus had asked them to say.

Peter and John followed the man to a large room upstairs. They looked around the room. It was ready, just as Jesus had said. There was a table in the middle of the room and places to sit.

Then Peter and John made the Passover supper in that room. When Jesus and the other disciples came, the meal was ready for them. Jesus must have been happy that Peter and John were willing to help. Do you think Jesus is happy when you help others?

"At the house he enters, tell the man in charge, 'Our Master sent us to see the room you have ready for us, where we will eat the Passover supper this evening!' He will take you upstairs to a large room all set up. Prepare our supper there."
Mark 14:14-15

Think

1. Which of Jesus' friends helped Him? 2. Why did they help Him? 3. What can you do to help Jesus? 4. What can you do to help others?

Learn

From this story we learn that Jesus' friends became His helpers.

Do

On a card, draw a smiling face on one side and a frowning face on the other. Whenever you a helper, put the smiling face where you can see it. When you are not, put the frowning face where you can see it.

WASHING DISCIPLES' FEET
Like Jesus: SERVING OTHERS

By the time Jesus and His disciples arrived at the upstairs room, Peter and John had finished preparing the Passover meal. It was time to eat.

Everyone must have been glad to sit down at the table. They were tired and their feet were dirty from the long walk on the dusty roads to Jerusalem.

Of course Jesus bowed His head and thanked God for the food before everyone began to eat. But Jesus didn't eat right away. He took a jar and poured water into a basin. He knelt by one of the disciples and began to wash his feet. Then He dried them with the towel.

Jesus went to the next disciple. He washed his feet and dried them with the towel, too.

The disciples were surprised to see what Jesus was doing. At that time, only servants washed the feet of others. It was not a job for important people, especially someone as important as Jesus. But the disciples did not know what to say to Jesus so they kept quiet.

Then Jesus came to Peter. Peter couldn't keep quiet. "Master, you shouldn't be washing our feet like this," he said. "I won't let you do it."

Jesus said to Peter, "If you do not let Me wash your feet, you can't be with Me."

Jesus washed the feet of every disciple. Then He sat down again at the table. All the disciples were puzzled. Why did Jesus, their Master and Teacher, kneel down and wash their feet?

Jesus said to them, "I washed your feet to show you how much I love you. If you love Me, you must be a servant to others. That is how we become happy."

Peter protested, "You shall never wash my feet!"

"But if I don't, you can't be My partner," Jesus replied. John 13:8

Think

1. What did Jesus do to serve His friends? 2. Who usually did this kind of work? 3. How can you serve someone today? 4. Why is Jesus pleased when you do?

Learn

From this story we learn that Jesus served His disciples by washing their feet.

Do

Think of one thing you can do to serve someone in your family today. Do it for him or her.

THE LAST SUPPER

Like Jesus: BEING WITH THOSE WE LOVE

Do you like to be with your very best friends? Do you like to be with your family? We often feel warm and wonderful when we are with friends and family.

The stories of Jesus tell how much He enjoyed being with His close friends, His disciples. Many stories tell about Jesus and His friends eating together. The story of the Last Supper is one of those special stories.

"I have looked forward to eating with you tonight," Jesus said to them as they sat at the table.

Jesus had many important things to share with His friends that night. He knew it was the last night they were to be together.

Jesus also knew something that made Him sad. "One of you will betray Me," He told them.

The disciples were surprised. Peter whispered to John, who sat next to Jesus, to ask who it was. When John asked, Jesus said, "When I dip My bread in the bowl and give it to someone, that will be the person." The other disciples did not hear what Jesus said. Only John knew the truth.

Jesus took a piece of bread and dipped it into the bowl, then gave it to Judas. At that moment, Judas was certain that he would go ahead with his plans to betray Jesus.

"Hurry and do what you are planning," Jesus told Judas. Judas quickly left the table and hurried away.

The disciples did not understand why Judas left. They still did not know who would betray Jesus.

Now Jesus was alone with the eleven disciples who were faithful to Him. He wanted to share with them the important things that they must learn.

Jesus took a loaf of bread and broke it and gave each disciple a piece. "Eat this bread," Jesus told them. "Like the bread, My body will be broken for you. Eat this bread often to remember Me."

The disciples did not know that soon Jesus would be away from them in heaven. Jesus was teaching them an important way to remember Him often. He did not want them to ever forget that He was God's Son and that He had died for them.

Then Jesus took a cup and talked with the disciples about that. "Each of you must drink from this cup," Jesus said. "This is like My blood, which I will shed for your sins."

We, like the disciples, need to remember Jesus and His blood. Every time we take communion, which some churches call the

Then He took a loaf of bread; and when He had thanked God for it, He broke it apart and gave it to them, saying "This is My body, given for you. Eat it in remembrance of me." Luke 22:19

At the Last Supper Jesus poured water from a jug into a basin to wash the disciples feet. Only servants did this kind of work, but Jesus became a servant to set an example of what we should do. This water jug was probably like the one Jesus used. It is made of clay, fashioned on a potter's wheel and hardened or baked. Most jars or jugs at that time were made of clay.

"Lord's Supper," we are reminded that He gave His life for us on the cross.

"I must leave soon," Jesus said. "While I am gone remember to eat the bread and drink from the cup as we did tonight. Keep doing it until I return so you will never forget Me."

Peter did not like to hear that Jesus was leaving. "Where are you going?" he asked.

"To a place where you cannot go," Jesus answered. Jesus was talking about heaven, but Peter did not understand.

"Let me go with you," said Peter. "I will even die for you."

"Die for Me?" Jesus asked. "Peter, before the sun rises in the morning you will three times deny that you even know Me."

Of course Peter was sure that would never happen. Jesus kept on with His teaching.

"Love others as I love you," said Jesus. "This will show the world that you are My disciples."

Jesus told them many things about His home in heaven. "I am going back to My Father's house," He said. "There I will make a place for each of you. Before long I will return and will take those who believe in Me to heaven. So you must tell others about Me while I am gone. Help others know Me by doing the things you saw Me do and saying the things you heard Me say."

After that Jesus prayed for His disciples. He asked God to take care of them while He was gone. He also asked God to help them share the Good News about Jesus as Jesus Himself had shared it.

At last the supper was over. It was time to leave. This was a night the disciples would never forget. And it is a night we will never forget either. Every time we take communion we remember that night and the things Jesus said and did. And we remember how much Jesus loves us, and that He will never leave us.

Then they sang a hymn and went out to the Mount of Olives.
Mark 14:26

Think

1. Who did Jesus eat with at the Last Supper? 2. What did He say about the bread and the cup? 3. How does communion, or the Lord's Supper, help us remember Jesus' death on the cross and that He is always with us?

Learn

From this story we learn that Jesus enjoyed being with those He loved.

Do

Talk with your pastor or Sunday school teacher about communion and what it means in your church. Ask your pastor to explain how communion is served and why.

VINE AND BRANCHES
Like Jesus: A SOURCE OF STRENGTH

I t was late that night when Jesus and His disciples finished their Passover meal. Jesus led His friends from the upstairs room onto the quiet streets.

Jesus had shared many important things with His disciples at the supper table. But He had much more to teach them that night. As they walked through the streets and across the Kidron Valley toward Gethsemane, Jesus talked about Himself and His home in heaven.

"I am like a grapevine," He said. "God is like the gardener who cares for it. And you are like the branches of the vine."

"When branches do not bear fruit, God cuts them off and throws them into a fire. When branches bear fruit, but not enough, God prunes them, cutting back so they will produce more fruit than before."

"If you obey Me and do what you should, you will produce much fruit," Jesus told them. "If you don't, that will show that you do not truly love Me. Then you are like the branch that has withered and died, and is good only to be burned."

"I am the vine that gives life to its branches. If you obey Me and trust Me, I will give you strength to grow and do what God wants you to do," Jesus said. "Then you will be happy and your life will produce much fruit."

"But how will we know when we are producing much fruit?" the disciples asked.

"When you obey Me and love others as I love you," Jesus answered."

Like a healthy grapevine, Jesus gives strength to us. Like healthy branches, we give strength to our "fruit"—those who need us to tell them about Christ.

"Take care to live in Me, and let Me live in you. For a branch can't produce fruit when severed from the vine. Nor can you be fruitful apart from Me." John 15:4

Think

1. What is Jesus like? Why? 2. What does He say we are like? Why? 3. What is the fruit that we are to bear?

Learn

From this story we learn that Jesus is the source of our strength, and we are the source of strength to those who know Christ through us.

Do

Draw five circles, like a bunch of grapes. Put a stem and long vine at the top. At the end of the vine write JESUS. At the stem write ME. Then in each circle (grape) write the name of a person you want to tell about Jesus. That person will be your "fruit."

JESUS PRAYS IN GETHSEMANE
Like Jesus: PRAYING WHEN IN TROUBLE

Through the dark streets of Jerusalem Jesus and His disciples went. They walked across the Kidron Valley, and up the Mount of Olives to Gethsemane. This was a quiet garden with a grove of olive trees and a large rock where Jesus went to pray.

He went forward a little...and prayed, "My Father! If it is possible, let this cup be taken away from Me. But I want Your will, not Mine."
Matthew 26:39

Jesus was greatly troubled, for He must soon die for the sins of the world. He would be punished for all the wrong things we have done. It doesn't seem right, but that was God's plan. If Jesus didn't die for us, we would be punished.

Whenever Jesus was alone or hurt, He prayed, talking with the Father in heaven. That's a good idea for us too, isn't it?

Jesus took His closest friends—Peter, James and John—to a quiet place in the garden. "Stay here and watch and pray," He told them. "I will go a little farther and pray alone."

Jesus went to a large rocky part of the garden, knelt on the ground and prayed. "If there is some way to remove this suffering, please do," Jesus prayed. "But do what You think is best, not what I want."

When Jesus went back to the three disciples, He found them sleeping. "Couldn't you stay awake for one hour to pray with Me?" he asked. "Watch and pray with Me if you want to keep from being tempted."

Jesus prayed again, this time so much that sweat fell from his face like great drops of blood. Three times He prayed, and three times He found the disciples sleeping. But the third time He woke them.

"Get up!" He said. "I will soon be betrayed." The disciples looked. Coming up the path were torches and the voices of many people.

Think

1. Why was Jesus praying in the garden? 2. What did He say to His Father in heaven? 3. Why was He suffering now? 4. What should we do when we have trouble?

Learn

From this story we learn that Jesus prayed in time of trouble. We should do that, too.

Do

Ask your Mother or Father to help you find a picture that shows Jesus praying. If you find one, hang up the picture to remind you to pray when you have trouble (and when you don't!). If you don't find one, draw a picture of Jesus praying, and hang it up.

JUDAS BETRAYS JESUS

Like Jesus: NOT HURTING BACK

As the disciples looked across the Garden of Gethsemane, they saw soldiers coming, led by Judas.

Judas walked up to Jesus and kissed Him so the soldiers would know who Jesus was.

Jesus knew that this man who had been His disciple wanted to hurt Him. He knew the soldiers would hurt Him, and the religious leaders. But Jesus did not want to hurt anyone.

"Who are you looking for?" Jesus asked the soldiers.

"Jesus of Nazareth," they answered.

"I am He," Jesus said.

The soldiers were afraid of Jesus. They had heard of all the miracles He had done. Now they were here to arrest Him, but they fell back in fear.

At last some of the soldiers had enough courage to take hold of Jesus. This made Peter angry, so he cut off one soldier's ear with a sword.

"Peter, put your sword away," Jesus said. "Don't you know I could call a whole army of angels to rescue Me?" Jesus did not want even enemy soldiers to get hurt, though they were trying to hurt Him.

Jesus touched the soldier's ear. At once it was healed.

"Do you need an army to capture Me?" Jesus said to the soldiers and religious leaders who were there. "I taught in the Temple openly every day and you did not touch Me. Why must you come in the night to take Me away?"

By this time the disciples were so afraid that they ran away. Then the soldiers bound Jesus and took Him away to be judged, even though He did not hurt anyone.

At that very moment while He was still speaking, Judas, one of the Twelve, arrived with a great crowd armed with swords and clubs, sent by the Jewish leaders. Matthew 26:47

Think

1. Who came to take Jesus away? Why? 2. What did Peter do? 3. Why did Jesus not want him to do that? 4. What could Jesus have done? 5. Why didn't Jesus hurt those who tried to hurt Him?

Learn

From this story we learn that Jesus would not hurt those who hurt Him.

Do

Can you think of a person who wants to hurt you in some way? Write that person's name on a piece of paper. Pray for that person now.

JESUS GOES ON TRIAL

Like Jesus: NOT GETTING ANGRY

When the soldiers found Jesus in Gethsemane, they bound Him and took Him to the house of Caiaphas, the High Priest. This man was one of the religious leaders who hated Jesus. The religious leaders wanted to kill Jesus.

As the soldiers led Jesus into the house, they began to make fun of Him. They blindfolded Jesus and hit Him with their fists. "If you are a prophet, tell us who hit You," they mocked.

After that, they led Jesus into a large room. The High Priest was waiting for Jesus, along with the other religious leaders.

These men tried to find something that Jesus had done wrong. But Jesus had never done anything wrong. Then some of them lied about Jesus to get Him in trouble. But Jesus said nothing. He would not get angry with these men.

At last the High Priest pointed his finger at Jesus. "Are you the Messiah, God's Son?" he asked.

"Yes I am," Jesus answered. "Soon you will see Me in heaven sitting next to God."

This made the High Priest and his friends angry. "Do you hear that?" the High Priest shouted. "This man says He is the Son of God. Anyone who says He is God's Son must be put to death."

Of course these men refused to believe that Jesus really was God's Son. They could see His miracles, and hear His teachings, and meet Him face to face. But they would not believe.

"What shall we do with this man?" the High Priest said.

"Kill Him!" said the others.

Then the men made fun of Jesus. They spit on Him and hit Him with their fists. But even when they did these mean things, Jesus would not get angry with them.

...Then the High Priest asked Him, "Are You the Messiah, the Son of God?"

Jesus said, "I am, and you will see Me sitting at the right hand of God, and returning to earth in the clouds of heaven." Mark 14:61,62

Think

1. What mean things did these men do to Jesus? 2. What did Jesus do to them? 3. How can we be like Jesus when people say mean things to us?

Learn

From this story we learn that Jesus would not get angry when people said mean things about Him.

Do

Tell this story again but this time pretend you are there instead of Jesus. How do you feel? What would you like to say? How would you be different from Jesus?

PETER DENIES JESUS

Like Jesus: LOVING OTHERS

When the soldiers arrested Jesus in the Garden of Gethsemane, the disciples became frightened and ran away. But Peter came back. Even though he was afraid, he followed far behind the soldiers as they led Jesus to the High Priest's house.

Peter watched as the soldiers took Jesus into the house. Then he walked past the woman who stood by the door, letting people into the courtyard of the house.

The night was cool, so some soldiers had made a fire to keep warm. Peter came near the fire to get warm.

Peter must have wondered what was happening inside the house. He knew that the religious leaders were probably saying things about Jesus that were not true. He knew that these men wanted to put Jesus to death. What if they wanted to kill the disciples too?

Suddenly Peter looked up. A servant girl had come near and was looking at his face in the light of the fire. She was one of the High Priest's servants.

The girl pointed a finger at Peter. "Aren't you one of Jesus' disciples?" she asked.

Peter was worried. What should he say? Now the soldiers around the fire were looking at him, waiting to hear his answer.

"I...I don't know what you're talking about," Peter said. He even pretended to be angry that she would ask such a question.

"I don't know Him," Peter snapped.

Peter felt sad and afraid. He walked over to the door of the courtyard, wondering how he could have said such a thing about Jesus. But before long another woman walked up.

"This man is Jesus' disciple," she shouted. Once again Peter denied it.

"I am not!" he insisted. "I tell you I don't know this man."

Then one of the soldiers looked at Peter. "You must be one of His disciples," he said. "I saw you in the garden with Him. Besides, you talk like a Galilean."

"No! No!" Peter said. Then he began to curse. "I have never met this man Jesus. I don't know Him."

Suddenly Peter heard a rooster crow. He looked up and saw Jesus crossing the courtyard. Jesus must have heard him say those terrible things.

Jesus stared at Peter as He walked by. Then Peter remembered what Jesus had said that very evening as they ate supper together:

She looked at him closely and then announced, "You were with Jesus, the Nazarene."

Peter denied it. "I don't know what you're talking about!" Mark 14:67,68

This street is called Via Dolorosa.
Many people think Jesus carried the
cross along this street to His
crucifixion. The street is more than
500 years old and is built over the
same type of street that was there in
Jesus' time. The buildings along the
street differ little from those in
Jesus' time. In Bible days, however,
the streets were about 10 to 20 feet
lower than the street pictured here.

"Before the rooster crows in the morning, you will have denied Me three times."

Peter rushed out of the courtyard and cried bitterly. How sorry he was that he had denied Jesus, just as Jesus said he would.

But Jesus did not reject Peter. Jesus still loved him. He knew that Peter would soon become a great preacher. Someday he would even die for Jesus.

So, Jesus kept on loving Peter even when Peter denied Jesus. That's the way Jesus is. Even when you and I do things that do not please Jesus, He will not leave us.

Perhaps you have a friend who has turned against you. Keep on loving and being kind to that friend as Jesus kept on loving Peter. Someday that friend will be glad you did this.

And immediately the rooster crowed the second time. Suddenly Jesus' words flashed through Peter's mind: "Before the cock crows twice, you will deny Me three times." And he began to cry. Mark 14:72

Think

1. Why did Peter turn against Jesus? What did he do? 2. Why do you think Jesus never turned against Peter? 3. What did you learn from this story?

Learn

From this story we learn that Jesus will keep on loving us even when we turn against Him or do something wrong.

Do

Think of three people who would never turn against you, no matter what. Who are they? What would you like to say to each now?

JESUS BEFORE PILATE

Like Jesus: NOT SHOUTING OR ARGUING

In Jesus' time the land where He lived was ruled by the Romans. So the Jewish people living there could not put others to death. Only the Romans could do that.

The religious leaders who arrested Jesus wanted to have Him executed. But they could not do it. So they brought Jesus to Pilate, the Roman governor.

"What is wrong with this man?" Pilate asked.

"He's a criminal," they said. "If He wasn't, we wouldn't bring Him to you."

Pilate did not like that kind of answer. "Take Him back and judge Him by your laws," he said.

The religious leaders began to shout angrily. "He's trying to start trouble," they said. "He claims to be a king."

Pilate looked at Jesus. He stood quietly, saying nothing.

"Are you a king?" he asked.

"Yes, but I have come to tell people about the truth."

"But what is truth?" Pilate wondered. Then Pilate went back to the people.

"I find nothing wrong with this man," he told them.

The religious leaders began to shout louder. "He's stirring up trouble in Galilee!" they said.

When Pilate heard that Jesus was from Galilee, he decided to send Jesus to Herod, who ruled Galilee. Then he would not have to judge Jesus.

Pilate watched as the soldiers took Jesus away. He still wondered at this man who would not shout back at those who accused Him. Perhaps He was a king!

So Pilate asked Him, "Are You their Messiah — their King?"

"Yes," Jesus replied, "it is as you say." Luke 23:3

Think

1. Who wanted Jesus put to death? 2. What did Jesus do when the people shouted at Him and said bad things about Him? 3. What should we do when people say bad things about us or shout at us and use bad language?

Learn

From this story we learn that Jesus would not shout or argue with those who tried to hurt Him.

Do

Revelation 19:16 talks about Jesus. What does it say about Him? What do you think this means?

JESUS IS CONDEMNED

Like Jesus: SILENT WHEN ACCUSED

Herod was glad to see Jesus. He had heard many things about Him but had never met Him. Now here Jesus was, a prisoner in Herod's court.

Wouldn't you think Herod would have asked a hundred questions about God and heaven? But he didn't. Instead he wanted to see magic tricks.

Herod did have a lot of questions, but they weren't about God or heaven. Herod just wanted to see another miracle and to know more about this strange man who already had done so many miracles.

Jesus would not answer that kind of question from Herod. He said absolutely nothing.

While all this was happening, the religious leaders stood by shouting lies about Jesus. Most people would have shouted back, calling those men liars. But Jesus would not answer those people either. He said absolutely nothing.

This was no fun for Herod or the religious leaders, so Herod mocked Jesus by putting a king's robe on Him. Then he sent Jesus back to Pilate.

Pilate had hoped that Herod would judge Jesus so he would not have to do it. Now Jesus was back before Pilate again.

Before Pilate could judge Jesus, he received a message from his wife. She had dreamed some terrible things that would happen if Jesus was hurt.

When Pilate heard about the dream, he was frightened. He was sure that Jesus was not an ordinary man. But what could he do.

Pilate brought Jesus out before the people again. "I can't find anything wrong with this man," he argued. "I will beat Him and let Him go."

"No, you must not let Him go," the leaders and those with them shouted.

Then Pilate had another idea. "I will let you choose one man to be released," he told the people. "Shall I let Jesus or Barabbas go?"

Barabbas was a murderer. Pilate thought the people would not choose him instead of Jesus. But they did.

"Let Barabbas go!" they shouted.

"But what about Jesus?" Pilate asked.

"Crucify Him!" they shouted.

"Why? What has He done wrong?" Pilate argued again.

But the religious leaders kept shouting. The people with them kept shouting too. Pilate could see now that it would be very

"...He is not guilty of any crime. But you have a custom of asking me to release someone from prison each year at Passover. So if you want me to, I'll release the 'King of the Jews.'"

But they screamed back, "No! Not this man, but Barabbas!" Barabbas was a robber. John 18:38,39-40

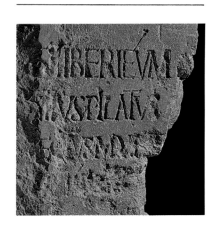

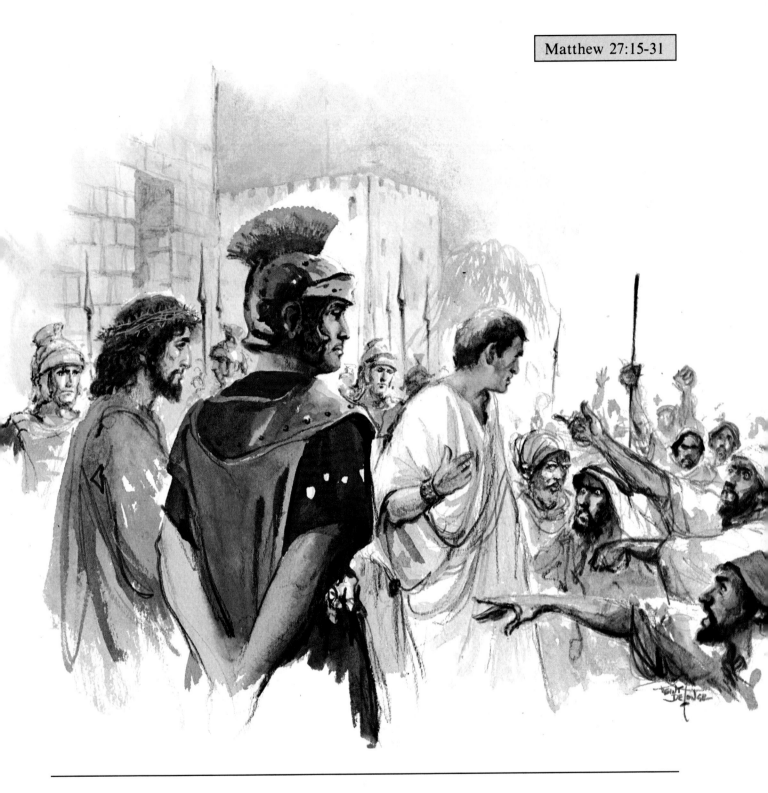

This large stone has engraved on it the name of Pontius Pilate. Only the letters "TIUS PILATE" remain. The stone was found at Caesarea. No one knows for sure the purpose of the stone except to honor the Roman governor who judged Jesus.

difficult to let Jesus go. But he wanted to try one more thing.

Pilate took Jesus into the fort again. He had his soldiers beat Jesus with whips and shoved a crown of thorns over His forehead. Then he put the king's robes on Jesus and brought Him out again.

"Look at this man!" Pilate shouted at the people. He wanted the people to feel sorry for Jesus and let Him go. But they kept shouting.

"Crucify Him! Crucify Him!" they kept shouting.

"YOU crucify Him!" said Pilate.

"We can't," they said. "The law won't let us do that. But you must crucify Him. He says He is God's Son."

This frightened Pilate even more. So he went back to talk to Jesus.

"Where are You from?" he asked. But Jesus would not answer.

"Don't You know I have power to have You crucified or to set You free?" Pilate asked.

"You have no power except what God gave you," Jesus answered.

Pilate argued with the crowd again, trying to convince them that Jesus did not deserve to die. But they would not listen.

At last Pilate had a basin of water brought to him. Then he washed his hands before the people. "I am innocent," Pilate said. "You are the ones doing wrong in having Him crucified."

"We will take the blame, and our children will take it too," they said.

So Pilate ordered Jesus to be crucified. Barabbas was set free. Don't you think Pilate must have felt sad to see Jesus taken to be crucified?

When Pilate saw that he wasn't getting anywhere, and that a riot was developing, he sent for a bowl of water and washed his hands before the crowd, saying, "I am innocent of the blood of this good man. The responsibility is yours!" Matthew 27:24

Think

1. Why do you think Jesus kept silent when He was accused? 2. Who wanted to have Jesus crucified? Why? 3. What did Pilate think of this? 4. What should you do instead of arguing or shouting back when someone accuses you?

Learn

From this story we learn that Jesus kept silent when He was accused.

Do

The next time someone tries to quarrel with you, say nothing. No matter how much you want to argue, be quiet! See what happens.

JESUS IS CRUCIFIED

Like Jesus: DOING WHAT GOD WANTS

When Pilate sent Jesus to be crucified, soldiers forced Him to carry the large wooden cross on which He would die. On the way to Golgotha, Jesus dragged the cross through the street until He could carry it no longer. Exhausted, He fell to the pavement which was made of large stones.

A man from Cyrene, named Simon, was forced to carry Jesus' cross the rest of the way to Golgotha. There on a hill outside Jerusalem, the soldiers nailed Jesus to the cross and set it up for all to see. Two other men were crucified with Him.

The religious leaders were there, making fun of Jesus. "You saved others, why can't You save Yourself?" they mocked.

From noon until three that afternoon the sky was dark. Then Jesus cried out, "My God, My God, why have You forsaken Me?" Then Jesus died, and the earth shook with an earthquake. The great curtain in the Temple tore from top to bottom. Even dead people who had believed in God arose from the dead.

The centurion in charge of the soldiers was afraid. "This truly was the Son of God," he said.

Near the cross that day Jesus' friends watched and wondered. Perhaps they remembered some of the things Jesus had told them about dying. But they did not understand that He would rise again from the dead. And they did not understand that Jesus was doing what God had sent Him to do, to die for the sins of the world.

But Jesus knew. And He died willingly, for that was why He came. God had sent Him to die to pay for our sins, and that was what He was doing.

Great crowds trailed along behind, and many grief-stricken women. Luke 23:27

Think

1. Why did Jesus die on the cross? 2. How many of His friends knew why He had to die? 3. Jesus wants you to accept Him as your Savior. That is why He died for you. Would you like to do that?

Learn

From this story we learn that Jesus did what God wanted Him to do, even though it hurt.

Do

If you have not accepted Jesus as your Savior, why not do that now. Ask an older Christian to help you.

JESUS IS BURIED AND RISES
Like Jesus: WINNING OVER DEATH

ear the cross when Jesus died, one religious leader silently watched. He did not make fun of Jesus, as the others did. This man Nicodemus had come to Jesus one night to ask Him about God, and he had learned that he must be born again.

Nearby a wealthy man named Joseph of Arimathea watched too. Like Nicodemus, he believed in Jesus but had said little about it until now. But as Nicodemus and Joseph watched Jesus die, they must have realized that He was truly God's Son.

Joseph soon made plans for what he would do. Quickly he hurried from Golgotha and made his way to the large fort where Pilate was staying. Perhaps as one of the wealthy men of the time he knew Pilate, so he could get in to see him easily.

"I have built a tomb for my family," Joseph explained to Pilate. "Will you give me Jesus' body so that I may bury it in my family tomb?"

Pilate sent for the centurion in charge of the crucifixion. When the centurion came, he reported all that had taken place that day. He told also that Jesus was dead and that they had not needed to break His legs to make Him die faster.

So Pilate gave Joseph permission to bury Jesus' body in his family tomb. Joseph hurried back to Golgotha were Nicodemus joined him. Together they wrapped Jesus' body and Nicodemus poured a hundred pounds of expensive spices in the burial cloths. That was the way people did in wealthy families.

Jesus' friends and family walked with Joseph and Nicodemus as they carried Jesus' body to the tomb. They gently laid His body in the tomb, and rolled a great round stone across the entrance.

But the religious leaders were still afraid of Jesus, even though He was dead. He had promised He would rise from the dead and they remembered and feared He would keep His promise. Imagine, they would not believe and follow Him when He tried to teach them. They did not believe He was God's powerful Son. But now that He was dead, they feared that His power might be from God after all.

The leaders went to Pilate immediately and said, "That man said He would rise from the dead. Order a seal on the tomb and put a guard there so His followers cannot come and steal His body and claim that He arose from the dead."

"Do what you want," Pilate told them.

When evening came, a rich man from Arimathea named Joseph, one of Jesus' followers, went to Pilate and asked for Jesus' body. And Pilate issued an order to release it to him. Matthew 27:57,58

The stone which was rolled across the opening of Jesus' tomb looked much like this. It was not easy to roll such an enormous stone. Usually there was a track carved into the stone floor at the doorway so that this rolling stone would stay in place as it was rolled aside.

So the tomb was sealed and guards were stationed there to watch. All through the next day and night the guards watched. They dared not fall asleep, for they could be executed if they failed to guard the tomb.

As the early light of morning appeared in the east on the third day, the guards were startled. The earth began to tremble and a blinding flash of light shone upon them. Then a person appeared, shining like a bright light, and rolled the stone from the tomb.

The guards fell to the ground, trembling with fear. It was an angel. But the angel was gone as quickly as it appeared and in the early morning light the guards could see that the tomb was empty.

The guards ran to tell the religious leaders who had put them there. "Here is money," the leaders said. "Tell people that Jesus' disciples stole His body while you slept. We will see that Pilate does not punish you."

So the guards took the money and did what they were told. They knew the truth, but told lies anyway so they would not be punished and so that they could keep the money.

But Jesus had risen from the dead. Never before had someone done that. Never before had a person died and then raised Himself to life again. Never before had someone won over death.

Jesus' victory over death is a promise for each of us. Because of His rising from the dead, we know that we will rise also. Death is no longer dark and lonely. Because of Jesus, death means life—life forever with God!

But very early on Sunday morning they took the ointments to the tomb—and found that the huge stone covering the entrance had been rolled aside. Luke 24:1,2

Think

1. What did the angel do at the tomb? 2. What happened to Jesus that morning? 3. What story did the guards tell? 4. How do you know that you will some day rise from the dead?

Learn

From this story we learn that Jesus rose from the dead, and we shall also.

Do

This fall plant a tulip or daffodil bulb. It looks dead and lifeless, doesn't it? But when a beautiful flower grows, it will remind you of Jesus rising from the dead.

A VISIT TO JESUS' TOMB

Like Jesus: HELPING FRIENDS BELIEVE

T he guards were gone from Jesus' tomb now, hurrying to tell the religious leaders what had happened. While it was still dark, with only the early light of dawn in the eastern sky, Mary Magdalene made her way to Jesus' tomb. Soon Mary and Joanna would join her and together they would put spices on Jesus' body, adding theirs to the hundred pounds which Joseph and Nicodemus had given Friday afternoon when Jesus was buried.

Mary Magdalene, Mary the mother of Jesus, and Salome had visited the tomb the night before, just after the Sabbath ended at sundown. But of course they could not get into the tomb to put spices on Jesus' body, for the stone was across the entrance and the temple guards had been stationed there.

So they would try again this morning. This time Joanna would come instead of Salome. Mary Magdalene arrived first, perhaps to spend some time alone there at Jesus' tomb before the others arrived.

Of course Mary Magdalene was startled to see the stone rolled away from the tomb. She hurried to the tomb and looked inside. It was empty! Mary was sure that someone had taken the body of Jesus, so she ran to the city to find Peter and John and give them the news.

While Mary Magdalene was on her way to the city, Mary and Joanna brought their spices to the tomb. "But who will roll the stone away for us?" Mary wondered aloud. It would take the strength of two or three men to do that.

When Mary and Joanna reached the tomb, they were amazed to see the stone already rolled aside.

These women ran to look inside. How surprised they were to see two angels in brilliant white robes, sitting at the place where Jesus' body had been.

"Are you looking for Jesus?" the angels asked.

The women were so stunned that they could not speak. "Why are you so surprised?" the angels asked. "Don't you know that He is risen, just as He promised? Now hurry. Go tell Peter and the other disciples."

The women remembered now that Jesus had told them He would rise from the dead on the third day. This was the third day after He had been crucified.

...Peter ran to the tomb to look. Stooping, he peered in and saw the empty linen wrappings; and then he went back home again, wondering what had happened. Luke 24:12

The aloe vera plant is thought by some to be the source of an oil called aloes. Nicodemus followed the custom of the time by mixing myrrh (another oil) and aloes together to sprinkle on the cloth that wrapped Jesus' body. This mixture was like an ancient embalming solution. It helped preserve and perfume a dead body. Nicodemus used 100 Roman pounds of the oil, which would be about 75 pounds the way we weigh things today.

So Mary and Joanna ran from the tomb to tell Peter and John and the other disciples. They must have arrived only minutes after Mary Magdalene had found the disciples. They shared what they had seen too. You can imagine the excitement as Peter and John and the women talked about these things.

But they didn't talk long. Peter and John and the women hurried back to the tomb. John ran faster and reached the tomb first. While he stood, looking in, Peter came and rushed into the tomb. There were the linen clothes that had been wrapped around Jesus' body, neatly rolled up where He had lain. Now John entered the tomb also and looked at these things.

Wondering what all this meant, Peter and John went back home with Mary and Joanna. But Mary Magdalene stayed behind, weeping there by the entrance to the tomb. She must have looked into the empty tomb many times, wondering where Jesus' body had gone.

Once when she looked in, she too saw the angels that Mary and Joanna had seen earlier. "Why are you crying?" they asked. "Because someone has taken Jesus' body, and I don't know where they have put it," she answered.

Just then Mary turned away from the tomb and saw a man near her. It was Jesus, but she did not recognize Him. She thought He was the gardener.

"Why are you crying?" Jesus asked.

"Because they have taken Jesus' body away and I do not know where I can find Him."

"Mary!" the man said. Suddenly Mary realized that it was Jesus.

"Teacher!" she shouted. "You ARE risen!"

Mary rushed toward Jesus with arms outstretched. But Jesus stopped her.

"Don't touch Me!" Jesus said. "I have not yet gone back to My home in heaven where My Father lives. But go tell the others that I have risen!"

So Mary ran as fast as she could to tell the good news that she had seen Jesus alive.

"Mary!" Jesus said. She turned toward Him.

"Master!" she exclaimed.

"Don't touch me," He cautioned, "for I haven't yet ascended to the Father. But go find My brothers and tell them that I ascend to My Father and your Father, My God and your God." John 20:16-17

Think

1. Who saw the angels in the tomb? 2. What did the angels say? 3. Who was the first to see Jesus alive? 4. How do we know that Jesus has risen from the dead? 5. Why is that important to you?

Learn

From this story we learn that Jesus helped His friends and family believe that He had risen from the dead. We should do that, too.

Do

Cut a circle from black construction paper to remind you of Jesus' tomb. Cut a picture of a beautiful flower from a magazine to remind you that He is risen.

ON THE ROAD TO EMMAUS

Like Jesus: SHARING GOOD NEWS

Two sad men walked from Jerusalem to Emmaus, a little village west of the city. They talked about the things that had happened the last few days, how Jesus had been taken and crucified. They wondered what this meant for them, for they had followed Him and believed in Him. But now He was dead.

As they talked about these things a man came along and walked with them. "Why do you look so sad?" the man asked.

"Don't you know what has happened in Jerusalem these days?" the surprised men said.

"What HAS happened?" the man asked.

"Jesus has been crucified," they told him. "He was a great prophet who did many wonderful miracles. We thought He was the Messiah, God's Son. But now He is dead. And just this morning we heard from some of His friends who went to the tomb that they saw Him alive."

"Don't you understand?" the man asked. "God's Word says that His Son must die on a cross for the sins of the world. Then He will rise again so that all who believe in Him can live forever with Him in heaven. That is the Good News from God's Word!"

Then the man taught them many things from God's Word.

At last they arrived at Emmaus. One man invited his friend and the stranger to eat with them. As they sat down, the stranger thanked God for the food. Then He took a piece of bread and broke it in two. Suddenly the two men realized that this was Jesus. As soon as they did, Jesus disappeared.

Filled with excitement, the two ran all the way back to Jerusalem to tell this Good News to their friends. The Good News about Jesus is worth sharing with our friends, isn't it?

"You must be the only person in Jerusalem who hasn't heard about the terrible things that happened there last week."

"What things?" Jesus asked.

"The things that happened to Jesus, the Man from Nazareth," they said. "He was a Prophet who did incredible miracles and was a mighty Teacher, highly regarded by both God and man." Luke 24:18,19

Think

1. What did Jesus tell the two on the road to Emmaus? 2. When did they know that the man really was Jesus? 3. Why did they run to Jerusalem? 4. Why should we tell our friends about Jesus?

Learn

From this story we learn that Jesus shared the Good News of God's plan with His friends. Then they shared the Good News with their friends.

Do

Think of one person with whom you want to share the Good News about Jesus today. Will you?

JESUS APPEARS

Like Jesus: TELLING PEOPLE HE IS ALIVE

T he two men from Emmaus could hardly wait to get to Jerusalem. They had seen Jesus alive! How happy they were to tell their friends.

"Jesus is alive!" someone said as the two came into the house where the disciples were talking together. "Peter saw Him."

"We saw Him too," the two from Emmaus said. Then they told the disciples about their walk with Jesus on the road to Emmaus.

As they were talking, Jesus suddenly appeared in the room with them. He had walked through the locked door.

The disciples were afraid. They thought Jesus was a ghost. But He wasn't.

"Peace be with you," Jesus said. But the disciples still could not believe it was really Jesus.

"Why is it so hard for you to believe I have risen from the dead?" Jesus asked them. Then He showed them the scars made by the nails in His hands and feet.

"Touch Me," Jesus said. "Then you will know for sure that I am alive and have risen from the dead."

Even then the disciples stood there uncertain and afraid.

"Do you have something to eat?" He asked. So they gave Him some broiled fish. They watched in wonder as He ate it.

Then Jesus taught them again from the Word of God, telling them about God's wonderful plan. He taught them that God had sent His Son to die for their sins, and that He had risen from the dead.

That is truly Good News, isn't it? Like Jesus, we must help others hear that Jesus is alive.

That evening the disciples were meeting behind locked doors, in fear of the Jewish leaders, when suddenly Jesus was standing there among them! John 20:19

Think

1. What did the disciples talk about in this room? 2. What did Jesus teach them when He came? 3. Why is it important to know that Jesus is alive? 4. Why should we tell others?

Learn

From this story we learn that Jesus helped others know for sure that He was alive. We should do that too.

Do

Look at your hands. Do you have any scars on them? If you do, the scars show that you were hurt. Jesus showed the scars from the nails that nailed Him to the cross. That said something, didn't it?

THOMAS THE DOUBTER
Like Jesus: GETTING RID OF DOUBTS

For some time the disciples doubted that Jesus had risen from the dead. Even when He stood before them in a room and showed them the scars from the nails, they still wondered. At last their doubts began to go away.

But Thomas was not with them when Jesus showed them His hands and side. So Thomas refused to believe that Jesus had come back to life.

"Unless I see the nail scars in His hands and feet, and put my own hand in the spear wound in His side, I won't believe," Thomas told the others.

Eight days went by. Still Thomas had not seen Jesus. Still Thomas would not believe that Jesus was alive.

One night the disciples were together again. This time Thomas was with them. The doors were closed and locked.

Suddenly Jesus appeared to them again. He walked through the locked door as He had done before.

"Peace be with you," Jesus said to them.

Jesus walked over to the place where Thomas was standing. "Put your finger in the nail wounds of My hands and feet," Jesus said. "And place your hand in My side. Stop doubting and believe that I am alive."

Slowly Thomas did as Jesus told him. As he touched the scars from Jesus' wounds, he was filled with wonder.

"My Lord and my God!" he said. Thomas must have felt ashamed now.

"You believe because you have seen Me," Jesus said. "Many will believe without seeing Me, and they will be more blessed than you." Do you think Jesus was talking about us?

Then He said to Thomas, "Put your finger into My hands. Put your hand into My side. Don't be faithless any longer. Believe!"

"My Lord and my God!" Thomas said. John 20:27,28

Think

1. Who refused to believe that Jesus had risen unless he touched the scars? 2. How did Jesus help Thomas get rid of his doubts? 3. Do you ever have doubts? Remember this story about Thomas.

Learn

From this story we learn that Jesus helps people get rid of doubts, as He helped Thomas.

Do

Put a nail into the bulletin board in your room or some place where you can see it. Write THOMAS on a card and tape it to the nail. This will remind you not to doubt, but to believe what God said in His Word.

A FISHING MIRACLE

Like Jesus: SHOWING OTHERS HIS POWER

J esus was alive! The disciples were sure of that now. But they were not sure when they would see Him, or how long He would be with them.

For forty days Jesus stayed on earth. During this time He appeared many times to His disciples and friends. He had much to do with the disciples before He would leave them and go back to His home in heaven.

The disciples were confused and frightened. They still did not understand what they should do. One day the Holy Spirit would come to live inside them and give them unusual power to do His work. But for now Jesus had to teach them and prepare them for that day.

Jesus would not go back to heaven until the disciples were ready to do what He wanted them to do. So Jesus appeared many times and taught many wonderful things.

During the forty days, Jesus appeared to Mary Magdalene near the tomb, to two men on the road to Emmaus, and then to the disciples in the room where they were meeting. He appeared a second time to the disciples, this time with Thomas there.

That all happened the first week after He arose from the dead. Then they did not see Jesus for awhile.

One day the disciples decided to return to Galilee, back to their homes and families. What had started as a happy Passover feast had ended in the crucifixion of Jesus and the confusing things that had followed.

So, tired and uncertain, they headed home. When they came back to the Sea of Galilee, Peter looked at the beautiful lake where he had fished all his life. He had been in business there for a number of years with Andrew, James and John.

Suddenly Peter blurted out, "I'm going fishing."

"We'll go with you," said his friends.

They climbed into a boat and went out onto the lake. Together they picked up the large fishing net and threw it into the water. The boats made a large circle, with one end of the net at one boat and the other end of the net at the other boat. When they finished the circle, they pulled up the net. But there were no fish. The net was empty.

Again they let the net down into the water. The bottom of the net sank down into the water. Then they circled the boats again and pulled up the net. But still there were no fish in the net.

Later Jesus appeared again to the disciples beside the Lake of Galilee. John 21:1

John 21:1-14

Fishing on the Sea of Galilee was done in four ways: (1) The hook, usually used by an individual. Jesus once told Peter to use a hook to catch a fish (Matthew 17:27); (2) the drag net, lowered from boats in a semicircle, which pulled the net together; (3) the gill net, a net left in the water all night and pulled in by boats in the morning; and (4) the casting net, thrown from shore by a fisherman and pulled in.

The disciples tried again and again. The sun went down and they were still fishing. Throughout the night they kept throwing out the net, letting it sink, circling the boats and pulling up the net again.

But each time the net came up empty. You can imagine how discouraged these men became.

At last the first light of early dawn came in the east. Then the sun peeked over the hills that surrounded the Sea of Galilee. It smiled upon the fishermen, still hard at work. But the fishermen did not smile back at the sun. They were not very happy men by this time.

Tired and discouraged the men pulled up the net one last time and headed home. There would be no good fishing now as daylight came. The fish would head down for the cool deep waters, out of reach of their nets.

"Did you catch any fish?" a man called from shore as the boat came near.

"No," the disciples answered grumpily.

"Throw your net on the right side of the boat," the voice called back.

The disciples were too tired to argue with this stranger. So they threw their net over the right side of the boat.

When they pulled the net up, it was full of fish. Suddenly they must have remembered another time when this happened.

"That's Jesus!" John shouted at Peter. By this time Peter also knew that it was Jesus. Peter was so happy to see Jesus that he jumped into the water and swam to shore. The other disciples followed, pulling the net full of fish behind them.

Jesus was waiting on shore with fish cooking over an open fire. "Bring some more fish," Jesus said.

When the disciples dragged the net of fish to shore, they found a hundred and fifty-three fish in it. Jesus had shown His great power again. Aren't you glad Jesus can do wonderful things?"

"Bring some of the fish you've just caught," Jesus said. So Simon Peter went out and dragged the net ashore. By his count there were 153 large fish; and yet the net hadn't torn. John 21:10-11

Think

1. What did the disciples do when they went home to Galilee?
2. What wonderful thing did Jesus do for them? 3. Why is it important to know that Jesus can do miracles like this?

Learn

From this story we learn that Jesus shows others His great power. We know He is God's Son because of these miracles.

Do

Cut a picture of a fish from a magazine. This next week put it on the refrigerator door. When you see the fish picture, remember Jesus.

JESUS GOES TO HEAVEN

Like Jesus: GOING HOME TO HEAVEN

A fter Jesus arose from the dead, He appeared to His disciples many times. He taught them many things. At last it was time to go back to heaven, His real home.

The disciples, of course, could not go to heaven yet. They had to do His work, telling the world about Him. Jesus had told them how to get to heaven later, by believing in Him.

"Believe that God sent Me to die on the cross for your sins," Jesus told them. "That is the way to get to heaven. Then stop doing things that you know God does not want you to do."

Jesus took His disciples to a hill outside Jerusalem. There He talked with them for the last time.

"Tell people everywhere about Me," Jesus said to them. "Tell them they must believe in Me if they want to live in heaven."

Then Jesus told the disciples how much He loved them. And He told them what to do next.

"Go back to Jerusalem and wait for God to send the Holy Spirit. He will make you strong and tell you where to go and what to do."

Suddenly Jesus began to rise into the sky. Higher and higher He went. Then a cloud came and the disciples could not see Him anymore. Jesus was gone.

The disciples watched the sky for a long time. Then they saw two men standing beside them, dressed in shining white robes.

"Why are you looking into the sky?" the two men asked. "This same Jesus will come back some day, in the same way you saw Him go."

So the disciples went back to Jerusalem and waited for the Holy Spirit to come. When He did, He sent them out with power to do Jesus' work. And He will do that for us too if we let Him.

Then Jesus led them out along the road to Bethany and lifting His hands to heaven, He blessed them, and then began rising into the sky and went on to heaven.
Luke 24:50-51

Think

1. What did Jesus say is the way to heaven? 2. What happened to Jesus in this story? 3. Who would come to give special power to Jesus' helpers?

Learn

From this story we learn that Jesus went from this earth to His home in heaven. He has given us His Holy Spirit to give us power to do what He wants us to do.

Do

Read this story again. How would the story be different if Jesus had died on the cross but had not risen from the dead?

CHARACTERISTICS OF JESUS TAUGHT IN THIS BOOK

Acceptance: Accepting Gifts, *Story 42*
Accepting New Friends, *Story 40*

Accusations: Silent When Accused, *Story 52*

Anger: Not Getting Angry, *Story 49*

Caring: Wanting to Help Others, *Story 37*
Caring For Those We Love, *Story 27*

Choices: Helping People Know, *Story 35*
Making Right Choices, *Story 17*

Compassion: Showing Compassion, *Stories 16, 33*

Concern: Concerned For Others, *Story 10*

Death: Winning Over Death, *Story 54*

Doubting: Getting Rid of Doubts, *Story 58*

Example: Doing Something First, *Story 7*

Forgiveness: Forgiving Others, *Stories 25,31*

Friendship: Accepting New Friends, *Story 40*
Being Friendly, *Story 38*

Getting Even: Not Hurting Back, *Story 48*
Not Shouting or Arguing, *Story 51*

Gifts: A Gift That *Will* Be Given, *Story 2*
Accepting Gifts, *Story 42*
Giving a Second Gift, *Story 34*
Sharing God's Gift, *Story 24*
Deserving Good Gifts, *Story 5*

Giving: Giving Because of Love, *Story 41*

God's Word: Helping Others to Know, *Story 20*

Good News: Telling the Good News, *Story 18*

Heaven: Going Home to Heaven, *Story 61*
Knowing the Way to Heaven, *Story 32*
To Live in Heaven, *Story 1*

Helping: Asking Friends to Help Us, *Story 43*
Wanting to Help Others, *Story 37*
Helping Others to Know, *Story 20*
Helping Others, *Story 26*
Helping People Know, *Story 35*
Helping People Who Hurt, *Story 19*
Helping Those Who Need Us, *Stories 14, 15*

LIKE JESUS

1. To Live in Heaven
2. A Gift That *Will* Be Given
3. A Promise Kept
4. Worth Waiting For
5. Deserving Good Gifts
6. Obeying
7. Doing Something First
8. Resisting Temptation
9. Leading Others
10. Concerned For Others
11. Respecting God's House
12. Showing the Way to God
13. Showing the Way to God
14. Helping Those Who Need Us
15. Helping Those Who Need Us
16. Showing Compassion
17. Making Right Choices
18. Telling the Good News
19. Helping People Who Hurt
20. Helping Others To Know
21. Helping People in Trouble
22. Sharing Food
23. Helping People in Trouble
24. Sharing God's Gift
25. Forgiving Others
26. Helping Others
27. Caring For Those We Love
28. Loving Others
29. Praying the Right Way
30. Showing Kindness
31. Forgiving Others
32. Knowing the Way to Heaven
33. Showing Compassion
34. Giving a Second Gift
35. Helping People Know
36. Willing to Serve
37. Wanting to Help Others
38. Being Friendly
39. Doing What God Wants
40. Accepting New Friends
41. Giving Because of Love
42. Accepting Gifts
43. Asking Friends to Help Us
44. Serving Others
45. Being With Those We Love
46. A Source of Strength
47. Praying When in Trouble
48. Not Hurting Back
49. Not Getting Angry
50. Loving Others
51. Not Shouting or Arguing
52. Silent When Accused
53. Doing What God Wants
54. Winning Over Death
55. Helping Friends Believe
56. Sharing Good News
57. Telling People He Is Alive
58. Getting Rid of Doubts
59. Showing Others His Power
60. Encouraging Others
61. Going Home to Heaven